THE IDES OF WAR

STUDIES IN RHETORIC/COMMUNICATION
Thomas W. Benson, Series Editor

The IDES of WAR

George Washington
and the Newburgh Crisis

Stephen Howard Browne

THE UNIVERSITY OF SOUTH CAROLINA PRESS

© 2016 University of South Carolina

Published by the University of South Carolina Press
Columbia, South Carolina 29208

www.sc.edu/uscpress

Manufactured in the United States of America

25 24 23 22 21 20 19 18 17 16
10 9 8 7 6 5 4 3 2 1

Library of Congress Cataloging-in-Publication Data
can be found at http://catalog.loc.gov/.

ISBN 978-1-61117-659-9 (cloth)
ISBN 978-1-61117-660-5 (ebook)

CONTENTS

Series Editor's Preface | vii

Preface | ix

Acknowledgments | xiii

Introduction: Peace and Its Discontents | 1

1. Washington's Character and the Craft of Military Leadership | 20

2. Origins and Development of the Newburgh Crisis | 43

3. "By the dignity of your conduct": The Newburgh Address
and the Language of Character | 69

Conclusion | 94

Appendix A: Memorial from the Officers of the Army | 105

Appendix B: The Newburgh Circulars | 109

Appendix C: George Washington's Speech at Newburgh | 115

Notes | 119

Bibliography | 127

Index | 137

SERIES EDITOR'S PREFACE

George Washington's farewells, and his advice about farewells, occupy an important place in American public memory. Students of U.S. history know of Washington's Farewell Address—although they sometimes misquote it—and some also know of his address to Congress on resigning his commission at the end of the Revolution.

On April 19, 1983, President Ronald Reagan issued a "Message on the American Revolution," noting that the day marked the bicentennial of George Washington's proclamation to the Continental Army of the cessation of hostilities between the United States and Great Britain. Noting that Washington's announcement itself marked the eighth anniversary of the Battle of Lexington and Concord, President Reagan quoted from the proclamation read by Washington from the the the steps of his headquarters in Newburgh, New York:

> The glorious task for which we first flew to arms being thus accomplished, the liberties of our country being fully acknowledged and firmly secured . . . and the character of those who have persevered through every extremity of hardship, suffering, and danger, being immortalized by the illustrious appellation of the patriot army, nothing now remains but for the actors of this mighty scene to preserve a perfect unvarying consistency of character through the very last act; to close the drama with applause, and to retire from the military theatre with the same approbation of angels and men which has crowned all their former virtuous actions."

President Reagan's message goes on to remark that long months of diplomatic negotiation followed the cessation of hostilities, ending at last with the Treaty of Paris on September 3, 1783. Reagan's brief and in some ways routine commemorative message uses the patriotic celebration of a military triumph as a generic encomium on liberty and the debt owed by the nation to its warriors, then less routinely notes the months of negotiation needed until "the blessings of independence, which were secured for us on the field of battle, became truly secure only when ensconced in a viable political structure." The celebration of a victory reminds us of the larger frame and becomes a lesson in civics, a turn that appears to echo the point suggested by Washington by turning the celebration of a victory into a call to "close the drama with applause, and to retire from the military theatre."

In *The Ides of War: George Washington and the Newburgh Crisis*, Stephen Howard Browne visits an earlier and, in his telling, possibly an even more important, moment in Washington's career, in a speech that "while generally well known [to historians], remains underappreciated as a key moment in the American revolutionary inheritance." In the spring of 1783, Washington and his army were encamped in Newburgh, New York, on the Hudson River. They had been at war since 1775, and most of this time the Congress and the States had been less than generous in provision of supplies and pay. Washington complained in a letter to his friend and former subordinate Alexander Hamilton of being fixed in a predicament between "the sufferings of a complaining army on the one hand, and the inability of Congress and the tardiness of the States on the other."

Browne tells us how close Washington's officers were to outright mutiny, with rumors that at the end of hostilities they might refuse to put down their arms until properly compensated for their service. This was mutiny and worse—a threat to the new Republic itself and to the authority of the civil government. In a speech to his officers on March 15, 1783, in the meeting house at the Newburgh camp, Washington saved the situation. This book is the story of that speech and how it did its work, offering us an understanding of Washington's public character—itself a masterpiece of rhetorical self-fashioning—and of the circumstances and contemporary understandings that had led to the crisis.

The climax comes with Browne's analysis of the speech itself, illuminated by his detailed account of the rhetorical situation and by a patient reading of the speech as it unfolds, showing how Washington spoke "not so much to impose a moral obligation on a refractory people as to invite them to become what they promised to be."

Browne's book brings us vividly back to that moment in March 1783, putting Washington's speech before us in all its drama and its crucial importance to the possibilities of an American future.

Thomas W. Benson

PREFACE

History tells us time and time again that on the day when the forces of civil government confront the forces of military might, no one knows what may follow. Americans, it is safe to say, have thought themselves to have escaped this moment: whatever others challenges we have faced, at least we have never had to deal with the prospects of a coup d'état. This view is very much mistaken. In fact we have faced such a crisis, *at the very moment* when this country announced its arrival on the world scene. That moment came in the spring of 1783 in a rustic meeting hall along the Hudson River near Newburgh, New York. That the crisis was resolved by the Commander in Chief of the Army of the United States by means of an address delivered to a roomful of restive and deeply disaffected officers should make this episode of particular interest to students of history, war, rhetoric—indeed, to all Americans.

I attempt in this brief volume to tell the story of what transpired on that day, to examine what was said, and to suggest something of what we may learn from the affair. My thesis holds that George Washington's Newburgh Address illustrates to stunning effect the power of human agency in brokering one of humankind's most persistent, most troublesome dilemmas: the rival claims to power of civil and military authority. At stake in this story are abiding questions about the meaning and legacy of revolution, the nature of republican government, and, ultimately, what kind of people we are and profess to be. These are admittedly large and frankly old-fashioned themes, and I make no pretensions toward a comprehensive treatment of them. But that does not make such issues any less vital, and they need to be confronted if we are to give a coherent and convincing account of ourselves. The Newburgh crisis offers us an unmatched opportunity to take these questions on. In the process, we will gain perhaps a reawakened sense of the role of rhetoric in the founding of the world's first modern republic.

Stories are by their nature selective and strategic, and this one is no different. What I have chosen to include in the telling will be apparent soon enough. What I have left out, underemphasized, or otherwise neglected can be explained only as a result of my own proclivities, limitations, and habits of composition. The Newburgh crisis was born of long-festering wounds to the pride of the officer elite; while we are not typically inclined to extend a great deal of sympathy to such a class these days, the wounds were real. More to the point of this book, the hardships incurred by Washington's officers, though scarcely unique or even all that dire, created the material conditions for principled resistance. These conditions in turn led to the crisis that reached its reckoning on the ides of March 1783. How the crisis was resolved—not through force but through a singular act of symbolic inducement—underwrites the account and centers, as it must, on the person of George Washington. Here some explanation is in order.

Historians of American culture, a conscientious and disputative lot, have for some time now felt themselves obliged to make clear their party allegiances. This is not unusual: most scholars feel the same need, and for perfectly reputable reasons. As academic interests surge and recede with the tides of time, there will inevitably be those who miss the old ways and resent the vague suspicion that their interests and methods are somehow dated or, worse, complicit in a discredited school of thought. Within American historical practice, some of these dynamics are evident, for example, in the tension between social and old-school political historians. A brief illustration: I recently attended a conference on the American Revolution held at the American Philosophical Society in Philadelphia. A magnificent gathering it was, featuring Pulitzer Prize winners, learned and lively exchanges, and a striking number of young scholars. In two and a half days of discussion, I do not recall the name of George Washington being mentioned once. Joseph Ellis, one is led to conclude, is right: His Excellency (Washington, not Ellis) just might be the oldest, deadest white male going.

We must not make too much of this, or at least I do not. The shelves still display the latest volumes on Washington and other Founders, and there appears to be, if anything, a growing interest in reading about great people doing great things. This is all to the good: those inclined along these lines get to satisfy their interests, and those who are not get more fodder for their own particular brand of battle. Let me at the outset state that I am not particularly concerned about these contests, indeed find them tiresome. My energies in this book have been expended, rather, in providing the reader an economical but instructive account of a very serious crisis, an event of great importance, and in analyzing how Washington availed himself of the resources of persuasion to resolve it. In no sense does this mean I have gone it alone: students of the period will note that my debts are conspicuous, notably to John Shy, Don Higginbotham, and Richard H. Kohn. In addition to displaying formidable erudition in their work, these historians have seemed to me exemplars of scholarship unbounded by provincialism or undue disciplinary constraint.

I hope for all this that my own disciplinary orientations are clear enough. Here, too, some clarification is appropriate. As a rhetorical critic, I seek to explain the ways in which the arts of address are employed to make a difference. The traditions of thought shaping this approach are old and sturdy and continue to be reanimated by new and provocative insights. My treatment of Washington's rhetorical art is ecumenical, but if pressed I would confess to a certain set of assumptions largely Aristotelian in character. By that I mean to suggest a resolute concern for human agents operating in momentarily discrete circumstances, bounded by context and faced with problems arising from these conditions. The emphasis tends accordingly to be on the pragmatic functions of language use, especially as they are applied to resolving exigencies at once objectively present, psychologically resonant, and capable, at least potentially, of being altered through the available means of persuasion. Such an orientation is, inevitably, open to question by those who would look skeptically at investing so much agency in individuals, in texts, and in persuasion thus understood. Fair enough: I can promise at this point only a good-faith effort to situate Washington and his speech at Newburgh within a manageable set of ideological and material considerations. At the same time, my working assumptions about the capacity of human beings to symbolically construct shared realities remain stubbornly in place.

Our story begins with a broad overview of the circumstances that gave rise to the Newburgh crisis. We turn then to a more detailed exploration of the man who would meet that crisis head on and turn it around. Here I undertake a character study of sorts—not because Washington needs yet another portrait but because this matter of character must feature so largely in any convincing account of his Newburgh address. Although I have tried not to belabor the point too much, I do hope to convince the reader that Washington needs to be taken seriously as a man of words as well as deeds—indeed, to press the point that words and deeds ought not to be so casually distinguished. The General was no orator, classically conceived, but he was capable of expressing himself in powerful ways. We then turn to the sequence of issues and controversies that helped shape a concerted plan to harness the officers' discontent to vested political ends. I have opted not to couch these designs in the language of conspiracy or treason; after examining the labors of others to unpack the often fugitive details of the episode, I have concluded that no such imputation is warranted. Finally, I take up Washington's speech of March 15, establish its immediate coordinates, and submit it to a systematic reading. In the process, I hope to provide readers a basis for reflections of their own on the precarious nature of civil and military authority in American life.

ACKNOWLEDGMENTS

I am grateful for the research assistance of Jeremy Cox, who may be forgiven if he never again reads another debate about half-pay pensions. Emily Michels Browne provided valuable help in documenting sources and bringing the project to fruition—thank you, Emily. Tom Benson, Dennis Gouran, and John Gastil each contributed, in his way, to whatever merits this book may be said to possess. To them I extend a special note of appreciation.

Introduction

Peace and Its Discontents

The boast of official integrity belongs not
to that man alone but also to his times.

Cicero, De Officiis *III. 22. 76*

THE RIVER

Washington Irving thanked God he was born on the banks of the Hudson. Thomas Cole hoped—in vain—to capture in oil its "wild and wondrous hues." William Cullen Bryant thought he heard over its "clear still water swells / The music of the Sabbath bells." Then and again, artists have found this region endlessly compelling, have gathered "Poetry from its legends / Hope from its History, and a consciousness of God from its Beauty." Those more prosaically situated, however, must reckon against such aesthetic pleasures certain competing realities, not least the Valley's remote and formidable terrain, its interminable stretches of sunless days and sodden earth. Winter does yield itself willingly along the Hudson River, and spring will carry the memories of hardship and danger, as it must. But here in the Highlands, in the quietest months, time and stillness may yet prod the imaginations of men and set conspiracy afoot.[1]

By the autumn of 1782, the Commander in Chief of the Continental Army had moved most of his army to the river's banks near Newburgh, New York. With Yorktown behind and peace negotiations ahead, George Washington might be allowed a long-overdue return visit to Mount Vernon or, at least, a moment's relaxation after eight years of unremitting toil. The General, being the General, would indulge himself in neither, for peace was still but a rumor and the British, after all, remained ensconced in New York City. The Hudson River must therefore be protected. Some seven thousand troops—nine brigades and regiments from New York, New Jersey, New Hampshire, Massachusetts, Pennsylvania, and Rhode Island—needed supervision, accommodations, and logistical support. To this end, Washington set up headquarters in the old Hasbrook House and gathered about him his officer staff, including Major Generals Henry Knox, Horatio Gates, and Alexander McDougall; Colonel Timothy Pickering; and many others of note. It was an illustrious gathering. It also comprised the core elements of an insurgency that would, in short order, threaten the very principles for which the war had been fought.[2]

The cantonment for now stood at the ready: grounds cleared, huts built, and supply trains established. But what, really, needed doing? The British, of course, had to be monitored; Washington accordingly ordered his commanding officers "to communicate with the greatest dispatch any information they may receive of movements of the enemy." In the event, little was to found in that way, and the Commander in Chief at length was reduced to resolving such conflicts as were bound to erupt among a proud but bored officer class. For the "honor of the service," Washington wrote, he hoped from here on out that "there will be no instance where vexatious charges shall be exhibited by one officer against another, through petulance or personal animosity." The troops were another matter. They were, for once, relatively well provisioned, and Washington did his best to keep them occupied tending to camp necessities, drilling, and participating in the occasional parade of arms and maneuver. Still, the men had by November 1782 demonstrated an alarming record of wayward behavior, roaming the countryside, pilfering from civilian neighbors, and generally making a nuisance of themselves. Washington was not pleased: "The enormities which have been committed and are daily committing by the soldiery, since we have quitted the field, are scandalous beyond description, and a disgrace to any army; they must and shall be corrected, or the greatest severity take place."[3]

Caviling officers and rowdy troops were exasperating enough—but only that. Few, very few, could then discern, in the short and waning days of the year, far more dangerous portents at work. Among the officers, especially, the rhythms of military life slowed just enough to provide time for reflecting on the past and anticipating a rapidly approaching, altogether uncertain future. Neither prospect could offer much comfort; indeed, if only one fact emerged clearly from those long days and nights along the Hudson, it was that a reckoning was coming due.

A winter of discontents, then. Before the season at last ceded its grip, the officers' resentments would find order, purpose, and voice in what was to become known as the Newburgh conspiracy. It would reach its climax in March 1783, in a log and stone building newly erected on the cantonment grounds. There, at noon on Saturday the 15th, the Commander in Chief of the Army strode to the front of a large room and confronted what James Flexner has deemed "probably the most important single gathering ever held in the United States." What then transpired must by any measure be regarded as one of the most riveting, poignant, and consequential performances in the annals of American political rhetoric. Washington's speech that day has been judged by leading historians "the most impressive he ever wrote," a "brilliant piece of theater," a moment, all together, "that may well have been the most dramatic scene of the war." It is the subject of this book.[4]

Why Washington's Newburgh Address and the conspiracy that gave rise to it have not previously been accorded full-length treatment is not clear. Why they should be is very much so. Scholars of the period have disagreed over details of the episode, and some have devoted more page space to it than others; but those who have examined it seriously all agree that the Newburgh affair raised—and settled—issues of the gravest importance. The questions involved could not have been greater, and everyone in that room knew it. Washington's address, as Robert Middlekauff noted, "suggested that the Revolution itself was at stake," as indeed it was. On that day, the speaker discovered a way to interpose himself between the competing forces of republican government on the one hand and military force on the other. No one else, it is safe to say, understood better or felt more keenly the nature of this contest, and no one else could have resolved it so decisively as George Washington.[5]

THE GENERAL

His Excellency was not, as great men go, especially complex. The circumstances within which he had to operate almost always were, but the manner in which Washington reasoned through them into action gives evidence of a mind uncluttered by doubt, certain of purpose, and literal in the extreme. Irony did not come easily to him. And, though capable of great passions, they do not seem to have warred with others or to have lingered at unhealthy length: when an emotion demanded expression, he granted himself permission to air it out. Thus relieved, he then moved on. By nature and training adept in mathematics, Washington did not indulge himself in abstractions; ideas were most real, more vital, when activated toward realizable goals in the contexts of lived experience. He counted among his friends and compatriots some of the most gifted political theorists of his age— indeed of all time—but Adams, Jefferson, Franklin, Madison, Hamilton, Mason, and the others thought on a different level entirely. By comparison he was unlettered, provincial, *practical*. Of this he was well aware, sometimes painfully so: he was not a great reader; he was conversant in English only; and, though given the opportunity, he never laid eyes on the European continent. He could not affect an air if he tried—which he did not—and though he enjoyed finery, good wine, and the comforts of Mount Vernon, so too he relished the soldiers' campsite, a bowl of nuts, and a good yarn.

So, though not complex by conventional standards, Washington was certainly not simple. What kind of man are we dealing with here? John Alden has observed that "Scholars have ceased to put gilding upon a wooden hero. It has become clear that [Washington] possessed an interesting personality." Yes, the General was interesting, but in what ways, and in what ways of interest to our story? Our search for answers must confront at once the curious legacy settled upon a man who, for all his seeming transparency, has been rendered nearly opaque by generations of ham-handed portraiture. As Marcus Cunliffe memorably put it, "Washington has become, not merely a mythical figure, but a myth of suffocating dullness, the victim of civic elephantitus," a "fanciful figure, in John Ferling's words, "as lifeless as the image of the man that peers out from the myriad paintings suspended on quiet museum walls." Our task, then, is to reanimate Washington: not by adding yet another layer of gilding but by allowing his essential qualities to manifest themselves and in hearing those who, in his own time, bore witness to the man and his meaning. Here we will discover what I take to be the heart of the matter and the basis upon which this book is grounded. The image Washington presents to us is a study in *character,* the lasting effect of which was to broker the competing claims of civil and military authority. This quality, this capacity to grasp the proper order of things and to act on behalf of that order, I take to be essentially rhetorical. That is to say: Washington embodied in his very person those principles upon which the fortunes of the nation rested. In the climactic moment of the Newburgh crisis, then, Washington so fused the speaker with the speech as to make them indistinguishable. The dancer and the dance had, at last, become one.[6]

We will have reason soon enough to delve more deeply and at greater length into this matter of Washington's character. For now, it is enough to glimpse, however briefly, the basic alloys from which it was composed. For assistance, we may turn to those who thought deeply and well about what Washington meant, as well as to more popular efforts to capture that meaning. Among the most perceptive of these was not an American at all but a French nobleman of exceptional and varied talents. The Marquis de Chastellux, working as chief liaison between Washington and Rochambeau, had grown close to the Commander in Chief. Several years after the war's conclusion, he published an account of his experience that remains an invaluable testimony to the American ethos. Here he sought to identify what it was, precisely, that explained the uniqueness that was Washington. He could not. Like many before and since, the French writer, officer, and diplomat struggled to arrive at any singular attribute that defined the man. To grasp Washington's character was rather to appreciate its composite qualities, its distinctive structure and equipoise of disparate elements. It was a matter of balance, and it seemed to rest, the Marquis reflected, "in the perfect union which reigns between the physical and the moral qualities which compose the individual." Washington thus represented in his self a kind of "perfect whole . . . brave without temerity, laborious without pride, virtuous without severity." This sense of the perfectly embodied disposition runs as a motif throughout the General's career, both while on the field and much later. It was left to Thomas Jefferson, fittingly, to offer up perhaps the finest expression of this phenomenon. "On the whole," Jefferson wrote, Washington's character was, "in its mass, perfect, in nothing bad, in few points indifferent; and it may truly be said, that never did nature and fortune combine more perfectly to make a man great, and to place him in the same constellation with whatever worthies have merited from man an everlasting remembrance."[7]

Popular paeans to Washington began seeing print scarcely after the onset of armed hostilities, picked up pace in the ensuing decades, and persisted well after he departed this world at century's end. For all their prolixity and their often partisan purposes, a striking number of such portraits point to this impression of embodied harmonies. Many admirers, it is true, sought to call forth Washington's essence by summoning the name of another: a Moses, a Cato, a Cincinnatus, and more. It would be difficult, indeed, to think of any other world leader so frequently denominated in this manner. But just as often the appeal to a given prototype gave way to a more comprehensive strategy, as if even these historical models were incapable of subsuming into one form the variegated qualities that made up the iconic whole. Thus one Virginian, still flush from the recent victories at Trenton and Princeton, advised his readers that, should "any one of you require the force of example to animate you on this glorious occasion, let him turn his eyes to that bright luminary of war in whose character the conduct of Emelias, the coolness of a Fabius, and intrepridity of an Hannibal, the indefatigable ardours and military skill of a Caesar, are united." Still, wrote a Marylander, such precedents could not suffice, for no one but Washington "ever united in his own person a more perfect alliance of the virtues of a philosopher with the talents of a general."[8]

Much has been written about the kind of character capable of eliciting this kind of prose. And, it must be said, Washington's memorialists seemed to have perfected the rhetorical art of laying it on thick; they too must bear some of the blame for plaster-casting our subject. We cannot, however, simply chalk it all up to the rococo standards of eighteenth-century panegyric. The truth is that people can be quite perceptive when it comes to grasping what is in their best interest to grasp: they knew themselves to be the beneficiaries of one of the more remarkable gifts in history, the arrival of an individual perfectly equipped to reflect back an exquisitely rendered, idealized version of themselves as rightful heirs to the promises of republican government and civic virtue. This, they understood perfectly well, was their great fortune; but we know that it was no accident. Washington's character was in fact the product of his life's labor, crafted in the forges of experience and attended to with painstaking care every step along the way. A quick study in all things, Washington set about from an early age to mold himself into an exemplar of Virginia colonial gentry; then into the commanding officer of the Continental Army of a people at war; and ultimately into the inaugural president of modernity's first great republic. Again, we will examine this process at greater length later, but here it is worth asking after the sources, materials, and ends of what might be called Washington's rhetorical self-fashioning.

Character for Washington was not so much a natural state as an art, a way of being and acting in the world by design. The qualities that defined him were cultivated, not given. They were the result of choices made, of disciplined management and strategic expression. In time they would mature into a fully realized and coherent set of virtues, but they were never allowed to remain at the level of assumption. Honor, probity, civility, courage: these were attributes to be treasured, of course, but never secreted, jealously defended and prized but most effective, most real, when put to work in the business of life. From a very early age, Washington seems to have understood that if he wanted to be adjudged a man of character, he would have to seek out and labor assiduously at the task. If he was not to enjoy the blessing of a European education, then he would look to family and to books closer to home. If he was not born into the highest echelons of Virginian society, then he would insinuate himself into that society through family connections, marriage, and the company of older and wiser men. Along the way, he learned not to spit on the floor, to dance and ride with the grace of an athlete. In the process he learned to demand much of himself and, in making good on those claims, to demand and receive much of others.

Character thus conceived was a distinctly public affair. Although we may find more familiar a sense of the term as referring to private virtues, its eighteenth-century meaning is very much associated with the disclosure of the self in and through the company of others. Indeed, one could be said to possess a given character only to the extent that one was seen to possess it. In this the concept bears comparison with the classical Greek notion of *ethos,* the rhetorical significance of which is made dramatically evident in virtually all of Washington's public operations. It helps us to account, as well, for what otherwise might seem inexplicable about such an otherwise guarded and restrained personage. For all his protestations, his alleged shyness, and his apparent aversion to publicity, Washington in truth gloried in the lights of acclaim and in the sound of applause.

The marches and parades, later the portraits, ceremonies, and levees: these were in effect rituals of affirmation that served to confirm, not diminish, his sense of self. For all his plaintive appeals to vines and fig trees, Washington drew his true sustenance from the spectacle of honor.

We observe, finally, that while such public validation of character was crucial, it could not sufficiently motivate or exhaust the energies required to sustain its force. Character in the sense embodied by Washington had to be forever in play, harnessed to the ends of something greater than itself. It was best understood not as a noun but as a verb, a form of action that resisted the solid stance and demanded action. In the earlier phases of his life, Washington discovered that the two most satisfying contexts in which to nurture and exercise such character lay in the professions of arms and politics. Character, of course, shapes and gives consequence to the success of both, but we must not assume that both demand the same sense of character. It is no small part of Washington's legacy that he was able to subsume within himself the respective claims of each and by this means secure the fortunes of a new republic.

THE PLOT

Before the speaker sat a formidable array of military leadership, men who had, alongside their General, endured much and sacrificed more. Some had been at the post since the outbreak of armed hostilities; most had suffered the inevitable privations attendant to the officer's lot. The talent was not uniform. A few were unmistakably gifted: Henry Knox, the beefy Boston bookseller, applied erudition to grit and wound up, despite obscure beginnings, deep inside His Excellency's circle. Others, certainly of merit, were never able to command Washington's confidence. Horatio Gates, the English-born hero of Saratoga, seemed bent on irritating if not outright antagonizing his chief, and the less Washington saw of him the better for both. Still others—the balance—featured that admixture of virtues and vices we ordinarily associate with military brass. They were in turn courageous and quailing, generous and mean, brilliant and dim. They got drunk and quibbled over perceived slights; they honored themselves and the cause for which they were manifestly willing to die.

But everyone in that room, whatever his background, his record or rank, had proved himself a patriot. If nothing else, the assembled officers were bound as in brotherhood by the common experience of battle, of defeat as well as victory; though all had surely despaired of the cause at one time or another, the fact was they had chosen to stick it out. They need not have: home was but a choice away. Still. This war, like all wars, proved longer than initially anticipated, and like all wars it inflicted damage not on bodies alone. Something very basic to the officers' sense of themselves, of their identity as officers, as men of honor to whom just recognition is due, was felt to be under siege and had driven them at length to this place, on the 15th of March of all days, to demand a reckoning.

How had it come to this? In the long and benighted history of warfare, few generals have enjoyed devotion among the officer ranks as resolute as that accorded George Washington. Surely this was not a day to rise against *him*. All things considered, the state of the army was better than it had ever been. By the General's own accounting, the men were tolerably well fed, provisioned, and housed: no blood-prints in the snow or gnawing on boiled roots. And, of course, peace was near, or so it was rumored. The enemy, in any case, seemed quiet and distant—had been for some time now. But there is always danger in leaving an army with not much to do, and the men had had plenty of time in those long and idle months of 1782–83 to mull things over. In the process, they came to learn that such discontents as they imagined were not theirs alone—that many others as well wondered whether peace was as much to be feared as war itself. The crisis of March 15 was born of concerted grievances: the officers', of course, but also of long-standing political and economic frustrations. These sources are ingredient to our story of the Newburgh affair and thus introduced briefly in this section. Together, we will see, particular forces within the army, Congress, and financial sectors ultimately vested themselves into a plot that would propel Washington to his finest rhetorical hour.

On reflection, the wonder is that the Continental Congress survived as long as it did. Its shortcomings were the object of unceasing criticism, not infrequently by and among its own members. Its reputation then fared little better for generations after the war, when it was construed, especially in the context of the Articles of Confederation, as an unfortunate but perhaps necessary phase in the march toward a more perfect union. Today, historians rightfully warn us against heaping upon that beleaguered body more blame than it in fact deserves. That is always good advice, but we can at least acknowledge that the deliberative body proved a fair reflection of the people it was designed to represent: ingenious, inconstant, persevering, and exasperating. For the purposes of our study, it is less important to itemize Congress's failures than to identify those sources of friction that goaded certain of its members to contemplate such measures as led to the Newburgh crisis. In this context, we are usefully reminded that Congress suffered above all from a crisis of legitimation, a chronic and almost unrelieved anxiety that, though charged with an extraordinary task to complete, it was time and again refused the means to do so successfully. The complaint had merit.

The Continental Congress was conceived as a means of facilitating reconciliation or, failing that, the transition to national independence. In these early phases of its development, it may be judged to have performed brilliantly. With actual war came new and unexpected demands on its time, talents, and treasure, and here Congress stumbled time and again. The problem was most conspicuously a structural matter, but it was psychological as well; together, these pressures squeezed the system near to the breaking point. Prosecution of the war demanded a unified, consolidated, and coherent source of authority. This Congress could not seem to manage. The reasons are not far to seek: the system was never really designed to superintend thirteen disparate, far-flung colonies waging battle against one of the mightiest militaries on earth. Those who sought—desperately—to set the federal government on a war footing faced obstacles on multiple fronts: states that stubbornly resisted usurpations of their authority, representatives who could not see beyond local self-interests, the endless shuffling of its members into and out of office, lax attendance, internecine strife, and, above all, Congress's inability to impose direct taxes to support the war effort.[9]

Inevitably, Congress's credibility suffered as it struggled to win a war for which it was singularly ill equipped. The result was a cycle of frustrations that was to persist for the duration, in which flagging enthusiasm and military defeat rendered the public even more skeptical of Congress's pleas for greater power. From such darkened circumstances, however, there emerged a select but powerful alliance bent on fundamental reform. This group, sometimes referred to as the "nationalists," aimed to seize authority deemed crucial not to military success alone but to the prospects of nationhood itself. But, though powerful, these agents of change needed friends. To whom would they look?

Americans were by no means a terribly straitened people. Excepting always the African and Native American populations, they enjoyed such natural resources and opportunities for growth as to make them the envy of the world—a fact that did not go unrecognized by the British leadership. By far most of this wealth was held in land, but still the colonial economy could boast of small but lively commercial centers and a robust export trade: all in all, a promising future within the Atlantic economy. War stressed the livelihood of many, to be sure, but it did not in general exhaust their wealth and in some cases opened up new if short-lived avenues for gain. The very real hardships endured by the army and the financial havoc experienced throughout the colonies were the result, then, not of widespread damage to the country's productive power; the real problem lay in a financial infrastructure rendered obsolete by the demands of war. The soldiers of Valley Forge did not go hungry, they did not shiver, because Americans were unable to grow crops, raise cattle, or gather wool. They suffered because colonial leaders could not yet figure out how to provision an army in the midst of plenty.[10]

Why was this so? The question requires a more complex set of answers than can here be provided, but a few reminders may help us appreciate how and why certain financial interests helped shape the Newburgh plot. The root of those evils besetting the American economy was, no surprise, money. Not, it must be said, simply the lack of it—though that was true enough. But even those rudimentary institutions of finance we would now look to, notably banks and private corporations, simply did not then exist. This lack of infrastructure, combined with limited specie circulation, formidable obstacles to transportation, and the extraordinary demands of a wartime economy, placed Congress and the country in a clearly untenable situation—but not a hopeless one. Absent the power to tax the states or the people directly, congressional leaders conjured alternatives enough to somehow keep the machinery of war gasping along. Foreign loans, such as they were, would help; forced requisitions of goods, though understandably vexing to the citizenry, might be useful in the short run; domestic borrowing in the form of loan certificates proved useful. And then there was the printing press, to which Congress turned for the emission of paper money—lots of it. Congress eventually flooded the country with nearly $2 billion of the stuff, "a revolutionary expedient," in the word of Don Higginbotham, "without parallel." It had to end and did, late in 1779; though these emissions had in fact served purposes of a sort, clearly Congress needed to secure other measures for funding the war effort. By 1780 Congress turned in desperation to the states and asked that they assume greater responsibility for the provisioning of the army. The result was predictably disheartening and could not have been otherwise. No amount of tinkering, however ingenious, could resolve the fundamental problem facing Congress: it simply had no genuine power to effect its will.[11]

If Congress and the public creditors had reason enough to complain, the army had more. Looking back over the long years of hardship and sacrifice, Henry Knox reflected that "Posterity will hardly believe that an army contended incessantly for eight years under a constant pressure of misery to establish the liberties of their country without knowing who were to compensate them or whether they were ever to receive any award for their services." Chronic problems of provision and pay had bedeviled the army since the onset of armed hostilities, and at no time throughout the long war was material support sufficient to the needs of either the soldiery or the officer corps. The miseries of Valley Forge remain most vivid in our shared memory, but Knox was referring to more than such isolated incidences of privation. Some stretches were worse than others, to be sure, compounded by the vagaries of weather and disease. But abjection born of human folly, of prejudices and penury, shortsightedness, avarice, and bungling: these were difficult to forgive or forget. No one was more alive to the absurdity of an army starved by the very people for whom it was fighting than the General himself. Here was an army, he wrote, "without any shelter from the inclemency of the Seasons than Tents, or such Houses as they could build for themselves, without expense to the public. [T]hey have encountered hunger, cold, and Nakedness. [T]hey have fought many Battles, and bled freely. [T]hey have lived without pay, and in consequence of it, Officers as well as Men have been obliged to subsist upon their Rations; they have often, very often been reduced to the necessity of eating Salte Pork or Beef not for a day or a week only but months together without Vegetables of any kind or money to buy them; or a cloth to wipe on."[12]

Hunger and nakedness, though serious enough, proved only half the problem. If we are to fully appreciate the conditions that led to the Newburgh crisis, we need to grasp the psychological as well as the material forces at work on the collective mind of the officer corps. These were, to put it bluntly, proud men. They came from diverse regions and backgrounds and professed different faiths and some no faith at all; a few were men of great wealth, most not. But they all shared an intense and abiding conviction that they had sacrificed their all to duty. They were, in the end, men of honor to whom honor was due. And what did they see? A people by nature suspicious of military caste; provincialists who subordinated the greater good to their private desires; people tight with a dollar but quick to make one at the army's expense, happy to receive the blessings of liberty but bafflingly resentful of those who secured it for them in the first place. And now, with peace in the offing, after all these years and all these sacrifices, still there came no firm assurance that these men of honor would receive their just due. And what was that? Not parades, to be clear, not even the accolades or undying gratitude of their fellow citizens. No: *the officers were hoping to get paid.*

THE SPEECH

America may justifiably boast of a rich and varied rhetorical tradition. For the most part, its leading voices are to be heard in movements for social reform, among communities of faith, and attendant to our rituals of civic affirmation. Of course, the realm of the political is almost by definition the space of the rhetorical: one need only think here of Henry Clay, Daniel Webster, and John C. Calhoun; of William Jennings Bryan, Woodrow Wilson, and Franklin Roosevelt; of John Kennedy, Ronald Reagan, and Barack Obama to be reminded of how closely the arts of politics and persuasion collaborate in the quest for public office. However different in aim and methods, these figures share a common genius for exploiting to optimal effect the resources of this ancient art. Chief among these is the public speech. By focusing so insistently on one particular speech act—Washington's address in The Temple on that day in March 1783—this study cannot help but raise questions about the explanatory weight it is made to bear. These questions can be rather complex, as it happens, and can be answered only by pursuing our account to its end. The reader will then have to judge of the matter. Washington's Newburgh Address nevertheless presents us with certain interpretive challenges, and they are best acknowledged at the outset.

First, it is not self-evident that any speech by Washington, much less one so brief and relatively untreated, warrants the kind of close and sustained analysis proposed here. A fair point. Let us admit that our speaker was no orator and that no one ever claimed otherwise. The General in fact seems to have had little taste and less talent for platform oratory; he appeared conspicuously reticent in deliberative settings, from his early tenure in the House of Burgesses through those tense weeks of debate in the Continental Congress and for the duration of his presidency. This is not a record designed to inspire confidence in a project that grounds an entire book on a single, short address.

Second, not only did Washington avoid occasions for public address; as a skeptic might observe, he was notably ill suited to its demands and, frankly, not very good at it. Here the claim is not so fair, perhaps, but offers a point worth considering. Casual readers will note in Washington's prose a certain labored quality, a stilted and sometimes awkward phrasing that cannot be chalked up to the alien rhythms of eighteenth-century expression. One senses the effort, as if the author had to remind himself in the process of composing what the rules were. This much, to be sure, is understandable: the lad was not favored by a proper English education—indeed had scarcely any schooling at all—and any comparison with Lincoln on this score would be merely invidious. Then, too, we are reminded that Washington's habits and occupations outside politics—surveying, the managements of his estate and land holding, above all his military career—were hardly the kind of activities conducive to the patient cultivation of verbal felicity.

Third, we need to confront the question of taking the speech seriously as an explanatory source. Is it not, after all, rather a lot to ask of such a brief and necessarily ephemeral moment to seek within its bounded idioms the elements of broad ideology, evidence of character, popular will, indeed the motive forces of history? This we might ask of a philosophical tome, perhaps, a political treatise, or even a rhetorical text commanding the stature of Jefferson's *Declaration*. But a speech? As it turns out, this question, though vexatious, helps us cut to the marrow of this project. Plato long ago voiced something of the same skepticism, not because he did not enjoy a good speech now and then but because he was afraid that others might forget that it was, after all, just a speech.

Such prejudices have a long and distinguished pedigree and cannot be convincingly resolved in these opening pages. I hope my accounting of the

Newburgh crisis in the end corrects their most obvious distortions, but here a few brief rejoinders may help clear the way to our subject. The aim here is not to assume a different posture at the outset; it is to set our coordinates free from distracting and untenable assumptions. For starters, anyone who has run his or her eye down the shelf of a good library will immediately grasp that we are talking about a man who spent an astonishing amount of his adult life communicating with others on a remarkable range of topics. Tens of thousands of pages of letters, orders, announcements, reflections, arguments, and so on make any claim as to Washington's reticence absurd on its face. Quantity is one matter, of course, quality another, and it would be equally implausible to view Washington alongside, say, Jefferson, or Adams, or even Hamilton. Still, we must at least acknowledge the authorship—in whole or in part—of the 1783 Circular Letter to the States, the First Inaugural Address, and the Farewell Address as genuine and lasting contributions to the American canon of political discourse.

As for Washington's uneasy relationship to the speaker's platform: it is worth pausing for a moment to consider a few facts. Excepting Patrick Henry, not a single member of the cast we refer to as the Founders felt the position of orator to be especially welcoming, rewarding, or comfortable. Aside from personal temperament, there were good reasons for such ambivalence, and the Henry exception helps prove the rule. The Virginian orator at once thrilled and startled the likes of Washington, Jefferson, and Hamilton, precisely because such power as he wielded threatened in each heated phrase to undermine republican norms of balance, restraint, and reason. Washington, like many of his age and class, retained a healthy caution about the orator's art, aware that the often uncertain difference between eloquence and demagoguery had done so much to upset the fortunes of past republics. At the same time, there is evidence aplenty that Washington possessed a keen rhetorical sensibility, that when the occasion demanded it, he was able to articulate his thoughts in "plain, unequivocal prose," as one scholar described it, and that he was in fact fully capable, as in the Farewell Address, of "fine touches of mastery, not to say poetry."[13]

There remains the matter of the Newburgh Address as a fit object for examination. We are, I think, happily beyond a phase in academic thought in which such focus on a single text was dismissed out of hand as a vestige of New Critical preoccupations or naïve objectivism. The past few years have witnessed systematic exegeses of Paine's Common Sense, Jefferson's First Inaugural Address, several of Lincoln's best-known orations, and speeches by Emerson, Elizabeth Cady Stanton, John Kennedy, and Martin Luther King, and results speak for themselves. To be sure, these are widely regarded masterpieces, texts of undisputed eloquence that gave voice and vision to the American prospect. Can the same be said of

Washington's Newburgh Address? Yes, it can, and I aim in this book to demonstrate why it ought to be thus considered. Along the way, I will need to involve many of the commonplaces one comes to expect of studies in the public career of the speaker, the familiar scenes and twice-told tales. These cannot be avoided—they are integral to and necessary for the analysis. What I do hope to offer by thus testing the reader's patience is a fresh and rewarding approach to the subject by taking what he said seriously, that is, by taking seriously the fact of the speech *as* a speech. By doing so, we will discover what is possible when character finds, at last, its finest means of expression.

A word, finally, about the speech itself. Those texts of Washington's with which we are most familiar were the result of considerable labor, forged over time and often composed with the able assistance of a Reed, a Hancock, or a Madison. And for good reason: the Circular Letter and the presidential addresses were designed very much with a broad and popular audience in mind and no doubt with an eye toward both immediate circulation in the press and, ultimately, posterity. For these purposes Washington asked for and received expert editorial guidance; though very much his own productions, the speeches nevertheless bear the unmistakable imprint of those more attuned to the craft of public address. The Newburgh speech is of a different order entirely. I will devote an entire chapter later to its explication, but here it may be useful to foreshadow that work with a few observations.

We have before us a speech delivered, in the words of James Thomas Flexner, "in what may well have been the most dangerous hour the United States has ever known." Washington had learned early in the week of several messages passed around camp calling for a clandestine meeting of officers. He moved quickly to head off that event by canceling it and announcing one of his own for midday Saturday. The General thus had but a few days to assemble his thoughts and put them into words. The result was an address of about 1,600 words, arranged into ten paragraphs; it would have taken perhaps fifteen minutes to deliver. The prose is not, with a few notable exceptions, especially elegant, its sentences often long and syntactically complex even by eighteenth-century standards. But the language is clear and forceful, the sentiments unmistakable, and the effect precisely what the speaker was aiming for. Herein lay the real art.[14]

Under the circumstances, the speech is as suggestive for its silences as for what it explicitly states. Washington, we note, refuses to lay any blame whatsoever at the feet of his officers; we find no talk of their guilt in the proceedings, no mention of any alleged role or complicity in bringing about the crisis. There is, in fact, very little at all in the way of speculation about who the agent or agents of such discord might have been, no anger or calls for revenge. On the other hand,

Washington does not downplay the seriousness of the threat, nor does he avoid the fact that the officers had real and pressing complaints. The positive work of the speech is rather to reestablish a moral order that has been for the moment unstabilized. To this end he exploits the occasion to stage a drama of a particular kind, wherein the officers are made to confront the competing claims of civil power and military might.

Hence my emphasis throughout this book on the word "crisis," for what we are able to witness through the address is a moment of excruciating portent, where historical forces have conspired to demand a choice. Washington's singular role in this drama was to orchestrate these forces, to give them meaning and direction, and finally to offer himself up as the means to their ultimate resolution.

THE LEGACY

The American Revolution, John Shy has written, was "a political education conducted by military means." The observation is characteristically astute and may readily be applied to virtually all major conflicts in the national experience. The sternest of masters, war has yet the potential to teach us who we are and what we may yet become. The lessons do not come easily: more often than not they are hammered out through a kind of second war over the meaning, motives, and obligations imposed by its legatees. The Revolution, no less than the Civil War or the Vietnam conflict, demanded of Americans that they come to terms with what had been wrought. We may think of this process as rhetorical to the extent that it has less to do with gunpowder than with the hard work of interpretation, persuasion, and consent. How a people ultimately choose to understand their war in turn tells us a great deal about that people. The Newburgh crisis may thus be read as a key moment in the political education of a people who dared now to call themselves a nation. And at the head of the class stood George Washington.[15]

What then shall we say of Newburgh's legacy? The question turns out to be rather more difficult than one might reasonably expect. Its timing, its assembly of notables, the drama, and the stakes involved would seem to commend the events of that March day to posterity and with it the rituals of nationhood and remembrance familiar to all Americans. But memory is by its very nature selective and self-serving, and Americans are not much given to reflection on the near-misses; bitter lessons, though swallowed, may well be forgotten. Not entirely: the grounds and buildings remain, the markers staked; a bit of tourist traffic helps out the local economy, and Newburgh will get a page or two in the latest volume on the Revolution. What kind of legacy is that?

Not much, frankly, and certainly not enough to sustain any real analysis. If we wish to better comprehend the meaning of Newburgh, to appreciate its importance as a chapter in the story of what it meant to become American, then we need to search beyond the lonesome statues and centennial blurbs. Part of our challenge involves us in the tricky business of looking for absences: no small part of Newburgh's legacy rests in what did *not* happen. Perhaps the most useful opening to the question at this point is to stress again the basic issues staged by the crisis and to observe how they played out in various postwar contexts. These can be only glimpses, of course, but they help illustrate the ways in which the Newburgh crisis made itself felt in the affairs of a very young people.

Early in 1783 Major General William Heath recorded in his journal "that a great uneasiness had discovered itself in the American army, on account of the great arrears of pay which was due, and some doubting apprehension as to the real intentions of the public to fulfill their promises to the army, and in particular that of half pay." That was, as we know, to put the matter mildly. When peace at length came, joy was mixed with the sour "apprehensions" of men and officers that the public was in fact even less inclined to entertain calls upon its pocket-book. Straitened New Englanders in particular resented the idea of endowing pensions for officers, smacking as it did of European traditions of indulging an idle and dangerous class of military elites. Such anxieties had a long history, of course, and nationalists in Congress had long been struggling to find a way around popular sentiment against various funding schemes. Shortly after the Newburgh crisis, that body did manage to pass a measure commuting half pay for life into full pay for five years. As its champions soon learned, however, securing votes for passage was one thing, actually receiving the funds and getting them delivered to the officers quite another.[16]

Public resistance to the officers' pensions ran along predictable lines of argument. The most vocal antagonists could indeed draw upon a well-stocked storehouse of complaints dating from the late 1770s: Congress had no authority to grant such pensions and no right to tax individuals or states even if it did; the people were already in desperate circumstances; and, again, such schemes played into the hands of the powerful and unscrupulous. Thus the good citizens of Acton, Massachusetts, applauded their representative for preventing "such salaries and rewards for public services as would tend to make government not a blessing, but an insupportable burden to the people." Like many such protests, the remonstrants happily acknowledged the sacrifices of and the honor due to the officers; gratitude was not, however, to be taken as license for indulging military authorities in a time of peace. As for pensioning them, they declared, "we cannot consent: the principles of the American revolution, principles so universally admired, forbid it." Other commenters pointed to the pensions as marking invidious distinctions between officers and the men, some to the fact that the officers knew what they were getting into when the war began. All seemed, like the good people of Dutchess Country, to fear that "such pensions will lay a foundation to enslave this free people" and that, in the end, the plan "would endanger the making of so many idle drones in the State hive."[17]

The Newburgh crisis was prompted in large measure by such fears of a pampered and privileged officer class. Those sentiments, far from ebbing with the onset of peace, in fact intensified in the years ahead. It could come as no surprise, then, that efforts among the top brass to organize a fraternity of former officers as the Society of the Cincinnati should come under similarly withering assaults. On the other hand, the idea was not altogether unreasonable. As Thomas Jefferson privately confided to Washington, "it was natural for men who had accompanied each other through so many scenes of hardship, of difficulty and danger, which in a variety of instances must have been rendered mutually dear by those aids and good offices to which their situations had given occasion, it was natural I say for these to seize with fondness any propositions which promised to bring them together at certain and regular periods." Jefferson, as usual, had grasped an essential truth, but he also grasped what many of the order's members did not: the Society registered as an alarm to many Americans who saw in it vestiges of European elitism and a direct threat to the spirit of republican government.[18]

Outrage came from every quarter, not least from among the retired soldiery. The Society purported to house the best and the brightest among the officer core alone, to thus set itself off from the rest of a freedom-loving and republican people, to ensure its own survival through hereditary membership, and to pose as the guardian of the revolutionary heritage. This the soldiers could not stomach. The Society may have nominated itself after the great Roman, noted one patriot, but did Cincinnatus "cabal and threaten to desert the arms, unless his country would promise him half-pay for life?" The Roman returned to his plow: could the same be said of these preening aspirants to fame? Did Cincinnatus "claim the merit of being the savior of his country, and wish to be the sole master of the labour of that people, and the property of that country, which he fondly imagined he had saved?" The events at Newburgh, still raw in the popular imagination, cast an exceptionally unfavorable light on those who would presume to corner the market on revolutionary virtue. Even the Freemasons, scarcely innocent of such suspicions, resolved to publically distinguish themselves from the Society. Whereas the former were devoted to republican principles, fellowship, and the public weal, the latter sought with startling arrogance to resurrect precisely the kind of nobility of the blood the Revolution had sought to vanquish. "The institution of the Cincinnati," declared one Freemason from Boston, "is concerted to establish a compleat, and perpetual personal distinction, between the numerous military dignitaries of their corporation, and the whole remaining body of the people who will then be stiled Plebeans through the community."[19]

Knox, Steuben, and other officers were genuinely taken aback by the heat of attacks on the Society and labored to amend its standards and public reputation. But they had utterly failed to gauge popular anxieties over their plans for what was, after all, a club for military veterans. That many did not see it that way at all testifies to how resonant remained the question of what role the military was to play in the civic life of the new nation. The slow but certain retraction of the army from the banks of the Hudson in the spring, summer, and fall of 1783 did absolutely nothing to dispel such fears. A final example of Newburgh's legacy may be found in the troubled attempts by Washington and others to imagine and implement plans for a peacetime military establishment. From our perspective, again, their thinking makes perfect sense: although peace had finally arrived, it would be foolhardy, to say the least, for the young Americans to believe they could survive amid the realities of an Atlantic world still very much in the throes of imperial ambition.

In April 1783 Congress accordingly appointed a committee, chaired by Alexander Hamilton, to consider the prospects of a peace establishment. Wisely, Hamilton turned to Washington for help. This the General was happy to provide, for reasons he made clear in a letter to Baron Von Steuben: "While men have a disposition to wrangle and disturb the peace of Society, either from ambitious, political, of interested motives, common prudence and foresight required such an Establishment as is likely to ensue to us the blessings of Peace, altho' the undertaking should be attended with difficulty and expense." Washington in turn sought the wisdom of Steuben, Knox, Pickering, and Clinton and produced, with his own additions, what Richard Kohn has described as "one of the great papers in American history." The "Sentiments on a Peace Establishment" went public in May 1783, addressing issues related to personnel, military stores, education, and the militia.[20]

The reaction was immediate, and it was not positive. The Massachusetts Assembly announced that it would not recognize Congress's authority to pass on so dangerous a plan, declared it unnecessary in any case, and lamented the very idea of "the grievous Expence of a formidable peace Establishment, which would inevitably ensue, if once a precedent for exercising so dangerous a power by Congress should be admitted." No one was more persistent—and shrill—than Elbridge Gerry, who with many others maneuvered skillfully to abort the proposal as quickly as possible. Congress had no right to create such a body, he insisted; the states were being asked to relinquish duly constituted authority; it would cost too much; it was not necessary; state militia were to be preferred in any case; and, above all, the plan was essentially designed to resurrect that bugbear of all genuine republics, the standing army. The presence of such a body, Gerry intoned, is "inconsistent with the principles of republican Governments, dangerous to the liberties of a free people, and generally converted into detestable destructive engines for establishing despotism." In time, however, "Sentiments on a Peace Establishment" would provide a blueprint for the United States Army, and its impress may still be seen today.[21] The uproar in this case, as with pensions and the Society of the Cincinnati, nevertheless serves as a forceful reminder that the energies circulating through the Newburgh cantonment could not be there contained.

In the pages ahead, I hope to show that the story of the Newburgh crisis is in part the story of America: of its birth pangs, its struggle to come to terms with what peace might mean. Hard choices had to be made, competing claims over civil and military authority brokered, and tensions resolved. At the center of this drama was its most commanding figure. After eight years of war, George Washington—and his new country—faced on this ides of March a reckoning no less severe, no less dangerous or full of portent. That he ultimately prevailed was no more a given than was victory over the British foe. But he did prevail. And for that we must remain in his debt.

CHAPTER I

Washington's Character and the Craft of Military Leadership

The Washington iconology is peculiar in any number of ways, but surely its tendency to immobilize the General is strange above all. The deliberate pose, the marbled aspect, the featureless monumentation: one looks in vain to Stuart, Houdon, or the Ladies of Mount Vernon for anything remotely suggestive of the man Washington was in life, in fact. He was in truth a gifted athlete, confident and graceful on the dance floor, a superb horseman, as a warrior indefatigable and intrepid. Why this figure should so often be rendered in stasis is explicable in part by the aesthetic conventions of the day—but only in part. Trumbull's *Death of General Warren* gives moving evidence that the age was fully capable of appreciating more dynamic modes of representation. The rest is mystery, for Washington was nothing if not a man of action. Even when still he was moving: no one could possibly write that many letters and missives, directions and complaints, without a nearly obsessive need to be always doing, always thinking, always seeking ways of pressing his will on the world.[1]

If we are to make any headway toward understanding Washington's role in the Newburgh crisis, this fixation on the stilled figured must be resisted, and aggressively. The challenge is formidable, the more so because we must contend against not only such leaden material renderings but generation after generation of verbal testimony to the great man's Olympian virtues. Hagiography has its place, and we can learn from it if we know where and how to look, but in this case it burdens our exploration from the outset. Like the statuary, paintings, and monumentation it mimics, such a legacy has the effect of fixing those virtues on a kind of timeless and immutable plane, where the vagaries of circumstance must give way to a product now outside history and thus, somehow, available to all and everywhere. "Death has put the seal to his fame," as a British writer put it in words grown, even by 1800, so familiar, "and his character and conduct will now be admitted to have been deserving of every tribute of praise which have been bestowed upon them. His coolness in danger, his firmness in distress, his moderation in the hour of victory, his resignation of power, and his meritorious deportment in private life, have established a name which will go down to posterity with those who have deserved well of their country with those who are entitled to be considered the benefactors of mankind."[2]

American audiences were treated on Washington's death to an unprecedented outpouring, more magniloquent and unrestrained than any before or since. We need not survey this body of panegyric in any detail to get a general sense of its tenor, but a brief sampling will help remind us that Parson Weems was scarcely alone in the work of deification. "His integrity was unblemished," intoned Oliver Everett to his Dorchester audience, "his humanity ever conspicuous and his benevolence unbounded. Neither in action, nor in suffering, did his courage, or his prudence ever fail." In Albany mourners recalled a man whose "Ambition was infinitely beneath the towering sublimity of his mind" and whose "pure heart was fixed on heaven." Bostonians were reminded by George Minot that "the whole desire of his heart, the whole pursuit of his labours, has been the good of his fellow-men." From Newburyport came reflections on the "robust vigour of his virtue," which, "like the undazzled eye of the eagle, was inaccessible to human weakness; and the unaspiring temperament of his passions, like the regenerating ashes of the phoenix, gave new life to the greatness it could not extinguish." And from his native land these words from General Lee: "Possessing a clear and penetrating mind, a strong and sound judgment, calmness and temper for deliberation, with invincible firmness and perseverance in resolutions maturely formed, drawing information from all; acting from himself, with incorruptible integrity and unvarying patriotism: his own superiority and the public confidence alike marked him as the man designed by heaven."[3]

Heartfelt, certainly, but the sentiments and sentimentality mount to the point where it is difficult to retrieve a sense of Washington as a living, struggling, succeeding, failing, and ultimately triumphant human being. We cannot unseal death, as the English memorialist had it, but we need not embalm Washington's life in the attempt. The important thing is to seek after not so much the product but the *process,* to rediscover, that is, Washington-in-action. The Newburgh crisis was a moment in time and place, beset by contingency, danger, and the drama of power. To grasp Washington as a man of action is to grasp how he mobilized the resources of self, how he gave voice to shared aspiration, and how he gave to that drama its full shape and meaning.

How best to proceed? At least two options suggest themselves, and, while opposed in obvious ways, they both deserve our serious consideration. The first recommends that we attend to Washington, if we wish to see him in action, as operating, as it were, from the beginning. From this perspective, we view the iconic figure asserting himself in those historical moments born of portent, at the outset, when all is new or seemingly so. This is the Washington of firsts—first in war, first in peace, in Lee's memorable phrase, and first . . . we know the rest of the line because Washington has been installed first in the hearts of his country-men and women ever since he emerged upon the world scene. It will be worth pausing, therefore, to reflect for a moment on what this angle of sight affords us and what it does not.[4]

There is, of course, every good reason to dwell on the image of Washington thus situated. No public figure in American history, it is safe to say, has ever bet-tered his talent for showing up at just the right time and place. The man knew how to make an entrance: at the start of hostilities in 1754 that would help launch an interminable war for great-power hegemony between England and France; at the beginning of continental gatherings to formalize colonial resistance. Wash-ington was the first of America's commanders in chief, its first president, the first to deliver an inaugural address, the first and only president to lead a military expedition in office, the first former president to pass from this world. These firsts are the more notable because they were made conspicuous, either because history conspired to make them so or because Washington himself made certain that his arrival onto the scenes of public life was duly recognized. That might mean writ-ing up an account of his early adventures into the Allegheny Valley, or donning his blue and buff uniform at the second Continental Congress, or riding into New York City showered with flower petals. But, whatever its form, his beginnings were designed for optimal symbolic resonance.[5]

That Washington could be at once complicit in this stagecraft and largely untouched by its more destructive effects was not a given. As an otherwise ap-preciative British officer observed in 1780, His Excellency may have been actuated by principles early on, but "Few men have fortitude enough to withstand the daz-zling glare of power, the love of which too often intoxicates the human heart, and where it takes possession, seldom fails to stifle the good affections which rise to resist it." In time, something like this very tendency would animate the partisan battles of the republic's first decade. But until then, most agreed that Washington entered on stage so dramatically because that was precisely where he belonged; when history thus beckoned, who could begrudge the actor his art?

BEGINNINGS

"We have it in our power," Thomas Paine famously wrote in *Common Sense,* "to begin the world over again." The sentiment is at once outrageous and thrilling; it is an arrogant and probably delusional claim on the power of human agency and a bracing insistence that human beings are not—must not be—forever fated to their past. The phrasing is classically of the Enlightenment, but the spirit it breathes is as old as human aspiration itself. To begin anew was the promise of the Christ child and of every revolutionary since; while debate remains over whether all American colonists believed themselves to be making the world over again, there can be no doubt that many certainly did. To the extent that we continue to accord to that momentous event the status of a founding, we are thus reminded of the enduring appeal of Paine's own declaration of independence. And since Washington is in some sense understood as *the* "Founding Father," we have warrant for further reflection on the matter of beginnings. Here, perhaps, we will find a means of ingress into his character and, presumably, the circumstances at Newburgh to which it gave expression.[6]

What is the nature of an act that is said to be an act that begins something? We can presume at the outset that because it is an act, it is by definition an expression of one's humanness. This is what Hannah Arendt meant to describe when she wrote of *natality* as ingredient to the human condition. A given action—in this case, the act of beginning—is thus at once sui generis and generalizable to our shared humanity. And precisely because to begin something is a human act, it can be said to entail certain moral implications. Acts in general and acts of beginning in particular by their nature are conducted under conditions of risk; a world marked by contingency and change ensures this fact. Such conditions invariably undermine blithe assumptions of stability or permanence. When we seek to begin something, then, we look for ways to give to our acts some chance of survival in an otherwise inhospitable environment. These provisions for the relative safety of our acts represent their ethical component, and here we inch back more closely to the matter of Washington's character and our access to it. When we seek to effect a beginning, we wish to provide it with some degree of security. We can do this by assuming certain obligations; these frequently take the form of commitments to *oneself* (I am acting in a manner consistent with my most fundamental and genuine beliefs), to *others* (I am acting in a manner consistent with your best interests), and to *the cause* on behalf of which the act is undertaken (I am acting in a manner consistent with my understanding of the principles at stake). Taken together, these commitments add up to a promise of sorts, as if to say: I promise that in exercising my power to begin, I do so mindful of the moral obligations thereby imposed upon me, and I do so not for arbitrary or self-regarding reasons but because the beginning I envision is compatible with our collective welfare.[7]

Such reflections may be excused, perhaps, if they prompt us to think more subtly about beginnings, their complexity as rhetorical acts, and the ethical contexts within which they might be best understood. I have suggested that this emphasis on beginnings offers us one route in our search for Washington's character and so a means to better grasp the role it played in resolving the crisis of

1783. The operative assumption here is that Washington's stagecraft was not only stagecraft, not merely self-aggrandizement and a flair for the dramatic. Probably some of these qualities were in play: the powerful can be as fully predictable as others. But the deeper principle holds that you can tell a great deal about a person in the act of beginning; such acts are disclosive: they reveal one's character and make of it an object of public judgment. They provide the conditions, ultimately, in which a person's ethical assumptions and responsibilities are made manifest. In short, if we really want to see Washington in action, to see how character works to get things done, then we need to see him in his beginnings.[8]

The merits of such an approach are not hard to find. Washington was in fact there at the beginning—so many beginnings—and he was keenly attuned to the symbolic potential beginnings represented. And when he acted to set events into motion, he could not help but disclose a great deal about himself, foremost his commitment to the integrity of the action envisioned and his sense of obligation to those who would be affected by it. Still, we have several reasons to be cautious about this approach and, without dismissing it, to ask after its limitations. First, to fix upon the moment of beginning remains a kind of seizure, and we are looking for ways out of that mode of analysis. Second, a preoccupation with beginnings can tempt us into ascribing powers of agency beyond the reach of mortal man—even and especially Washington's. It is telling, in this regard, to note how often the young Virginian is credited with—or blamed for—unleashing the furies of global war through his clumsy handling of the Jumonville affair in 1754. Thus Horace Walpole: "The volley fired by a young Virginian in the backwoods of America set the world afire." This is nonsense, of course—Washington no more started the Seven Years War than Gavrilo Princip started the Great War—but the point here is to mind the boundary where emphasis on individual action shades into the vexed territory of causation and influence. Nevertheless: a strong sense of beginnings gives us a means to see Washington in action, and it helps us identify moral commitments basic to his character. This much we will hold onto for the analysis ahead.[9]

ENDINGS

Andrew Jackson was not, in the ordinary sense of things, a man given to reflection. But he could be astute, and, standing on thresholds of his own in 1825, he offered up a telling comment on the only general more famous than he. "Both the surrender of his sword to Congress at the termination of the Revolutionary War, and his relinquishment of the Presidency," Jackson wrote of Washington, "are imperishable monuments of self-conquest, from which future generations will learn how vain is the fame of the Warrior or the renown of the Statesman, when built upon the ruins and subjection of a country." An imperishable monument of self-conquest: this Jackson never was nor would ever be, but the insight is both his own and basic to the received wisdom on Washington's legacy. It bespeaks a keen appreciation for that rarest of human traits: the capacity to cede power when one is most in possession of it. We are thus reminded that while beginnings may be one way to read Washington's character, surely endings offer another, for if the man knew better than most how to enter the room, none excelled him in leaving it.[10]

The proposition is promising: how a person manages the various endings and exits of life, reaches closure, as we might put it today, can say a great deal about that person. Certainly Washington's contemporaries thought so, friends and even rivals who seemed to have an especially well-developed taste for the art of leave-taking. Not surprisingly, the General's talent along these lines encouraged a robust cottage industry devoted to the cultivation of his image as an American Cincinnatus, the warrior returning to his plow, the statesman to his vine and fig tree. This is fair. One cannot help but be struck by how much symbolic charge Washington was able to coax from those moments when he stepped off the stage: of Mount Vernon, of Congress, of the battlefield, of the presidency, of life itself. The final Circular to the States at war's end, the yielding of his commission, the Farewell Address: it is hardly coincidental that among the most memorable of Washington's productions are precisely those designed not just to announce his departure but to do so with maximum rhetorical efffect.[11]

And it worked. George III is reputed to have declared that, should Washington indeed repair to his crops after final victory in battle, "he will be the greatest man alive." Modern historians, less given to saying such things, are nevertheless increasingly impressed by how assiduously Washington shaped to strategic ends his own endings. Garry Wills, among others, has observed that Washington proved to be "a virtuoso of resignations," who in time "perfected the art of power by giving it away." Similarly, Joseph Ellis claims—a bit extravagantly—that "Washington's extraordinary reputation rested less on his prudent exercise of power than on his dramatic flair at surrendering it. He was, in fact, a veritable virtuoso of exits." We do not typically think of Washington, the object of so much artistic labor, as himself an artist. In fact he was exquisitely attuned to the aesthetics of the exit, and we may learn much by asking after its assumptions, structure, and implications.[12]

We have established that a focus on beginnings offers us a means of access to Washington's character. Its essence we discovered to lie in the form of a promise, which may be taken to represent the moral content of the act. Turning now to its counterpart—endings—we are in a position to observe at the outset several interesting ways in which beginnings and endings are attuned to each other. We note, for example, that endings and beginnings hold a number of elements in common; though opposed in obvious ways, both nonetheless lend themselves to ritual, thus to display and its attendant stagecraft. Endings and beginnings together mark the space of the liminal, notably between the private and the public. Both presume a degree of historical consciousness and entail strategic interventions into the course of events. And both, we find, function as media of disclosure, wherein may be discerned the workings of character and its moral exercise.

But endings are of course categorically different from beginnings, and here we may pause and determine what is gained by fixing on the subject. Some advantage may be gained by stressing early the point that endings are not to be understood in the negative—as portending absence only—but are to be seen as performing tasks to which they are distinctively suited. Endings in this sense are not given but made; they are constructed and thus made to bear the imprint of their creator.

Washington took his leave on several and on very different occasions. But, like all such managed exits, his were bound by a set of assumptions basic to the art; from these assumptions we can chart our course to a better grasp of the character at work in Newburgh. To publicly mark the end of a series of actions is first to assume that such actions are of a class in which an end is possible and, in the context, meaningful. If this appears too obvious on its face, we have only to consider the vexed history of armed conflict in the twentieth and twenty-first centuries. Regrettably, the very concept of a decisive, authorized, and mutually agreed-upon termination of hostilities threatens now to go the way of . . . declaring wars. One need not be a modern diplomat, in any case, to appreciate how complex and elusive can be the art stopping what one has played a role in beginning. The Newburgh crisis puts this kind of assumption to the war's most severe test, at precisely that moment when it was not at all clear to many where and under what conditions war was to end and peace begin. That it turned out the way it did is explicable in large part because Washington understood that some things, at least, must come to an end.[13]

Left alone, the assumption that certain actions must be terminated is incomplete without an accompanying sense of the conditions under which the ending is appropriately effected. Classically conceived, this kind of understanding was explained with reference to *kairos,* or a strategic grasp of timing, and to *prepon,* a strategic grasp of place. To seek the (successful) end to a course of actions, then, is to suppose that it must be undertaken with a heightened sense of the immediate situation and in view of a complex array of exigencies. It was to this that Thomas Jefferson referred when he wrote of Washington: "Perhaps the strongest feature of his character was prudence, never acting until every circumstance, every consideration, was maturely weighted; refraining if he say a doubt, but, when once decided, going through with his purpose what ever obstacles opposed." End, yes: but to end well, know when, where, and how.[14]

From these assumptions we can proceed to ask just what kind of positive work such endings perform. My answer is that endings in the manner of Washington's may be taken as a form of gift-giving, the yielding up of what was once one's own to others for the common good. To get at the point at little closer, it might help to adjust our conventional sense of the phrase "leave-taking" and its variants. My thesis suggests that the phrase, in this context at least, is misleading; it implies a gathering up of one's self and a departure from the scene of action. The sense I wish to foreground, rather, insists that, under certain conditions, the act of leaving is made meaningful precisely by what remains with—is given to— that scene of action. We are known not so much by the fact *that* we left but by *what* we left. And that *what* is the gift. Now, implicit in this act of gift-giving is the message that the gift, having been created through one's actions, is itself worthy of giving, that it now has such value as to commend itself to the common wealth.

The act of an ending, properly staged, is thus not reducible to making absent that which was once present. To the contrary, such endings are the enabling conditions under which new possibilities are brought into being. When, for example, Washington relinquished his sword on that December day in Annapolis, he in effect bestowed upon his fellow Americans a new and valuable thing, a gift in the form of a republic, now relieved of its acute military burden. Embedded in that act, but not buried, was the assumption that what had been nurtured under one form of authority was now strong enough, whole enough, and right enough to enter the common trust. To relieve oneself of agency in this circumstance is not to declare a job well done and there's an end to it—to renounce further responsibility —but to give up what might be thought one's own but must, in the end, become the shared prize of all. This, Washington's countrymen knew, was the essence of virtue, the fullest expression of which is to yield power rightfully held to those now capable of wielding it rightly.

BETWEEN THE END AND THE BEGINNING
Becoming George Washington

In January 1754 a very young, very tired George Washington returned to Williamsburg, Virginia, after an epic four-and-a-half-month journey. He had been commissioned by Governor Robert Dinwiddie late in the previous year to deliver a letter of warning to Jacques Legardeur de Saint-Pierre at Fort Le Boeuf, ordering the French forces to relinquish their pretentions to the Ohio Valley. The French commander, predictably, chose not to obey the directive. But all was not lost: throughout the thousand-mile journey Washington had been keeping a sharp eye on—and a written record of—everything from the disposition of arms to Indian attitudes to the region's potential for white settlement. This kind of information was rare and useful enough, thought Dinwiddie, to warrant having Washington's account made available in published form for the members of the House of Burgesses and for anyone else interested in the rapidly unfolding developments on the frontier. The result was *The Journal of Major George Washington* (1754). The author had not the time to edit or otherwise tidy up the prose, Washington notes, nor "was I apprised, or did in the least conceive, when I wrote this for his Honour's Perusal, that it ever would be published, or even have more than a cursory Reading; till I was informed, at the Meeting of the present General Assembly, that it was already in the Press."[15]

The comment, though brief, is telling and provides us with a certain perspective on Washington's early maturation. We detect immediately the note of diffidence, an apology of sorts for the artlessness of his efforts. *The Journal* was perforce a hurried production, composed amid endless hardships and delivered at a moment of utter exhaustion. We learn, too, that Washington had not even been aware that it was to be published. Quite to his surprise, what were once private impressions had somehow become the provenance of a wider world. In the event, readers from Williamsburg to London soon learned of the harrowing journey and a good deal more about rich resources of the Ohio River Valley. But most of all they learned of George Washington. Fortune seemed to have ushered the young Captain safely home, and Fate to have commended him to the attention of history. That Washington had angled for the appointment in the first place, that he had taken it upon himself to gather those notes at all, and that he accepted the plaudits, remuneration, and advance in rank that soon came his way: so much is not typically dwelled upon. But the fact is that Washington was at the time intensely ambitious of fame: he was willing to undergo extraordinary hardship to get it, and he wanted always to be in a position to capitalize on such renown as could be gathered along the way.[16]

These traits must be kept in mind as we seek to chart the growth and development of Washington's character. The point is not to bring him down a notch or two: ambition and its attendant longings are scarcely unique to him, nor are they necessarily even shortcomings. To be mindful of Washington's driving passions in this early phase, rather, is to acknowledge the affective dimensions of his struggle toward full adulthood. Now, to get close enough, to see and hear and feel its energies, we need to drop in on him unexpectedly, where candor may be assumed and the guards lowered, if only a bit. The Washington correspondence affords any number of opportunities to this end, but for the purposes of this chapter we will pay the young man a visit not so long after his northern adventure, when Fortune and Fate turned out to be rather more complicated than he may have expected. Here we find Washington where we want him: poised between endings and beginnings, between youth and manhood, after the horrors of Fort Necessity and before the even greater horrors of the Braddock campaign. We will not see Washington at his most edifying—he could be, in the words of one historian, a "hot-tempered, fawning, reckless, young court pleader." But we will see him wrestling with the very grown-up questions of what it means to make a promise, of which motives must be adjudged worthy and which not, of the difference between acclaim and merit. We find him, in brief, discovering what it will take for him to become the man he hopes to become.[17]

The Le Boeuf expedition, a failure in one sense, rapidly proved to pay dividends in another. Washington's military career was quickly thereafter launched with his promotion by Governor Dinwiddie to Lieutenant Colonel of the Virginia Regiment in spring of 1754. And for good reason: anxious over the expansionist designs of the French in the Ohio Country, Dinwiddie had resolved to send the young warrior, accompanied by around 150 colonists and Indians, to beat back French efforts to construct a fort near present-day Pittsburgh. Setting out in mid-March, Washington and his men reached Wills Creek a month later and pushed on toward their objective. Luck of a kind came their way when, on May 28, the contingent ambushed a small force south of what was to become Fort Duquesne. The result: ten French dead, among them, notably, Joseph Coulon de Jumonville, commanding officer. If it all seemed too easy, it was.[18]

Flushed with "victory," Washington dashed off a letter to his brother, crowing that here he first "heard the bullets whistle, and believe me, there is something charming in the sound." Charm is a fleeting thing. Jumonville was not looking for a fight; nor, for that matter, were England and France as yet officially belligerents. The French (but not the French alone) viewed Jumonville's death as an assassination and the entire episode as an outrage. Vengeance was to be had, of course, and soon enough the commander's brother, Louis Coulon de Villier, led his forces against Washington and British regulars under James Mackay at Bear Meadows on July 3–4. There the men had constructed what can only with charity be referred to as a fort: after the second day of battle under truly wretched conditions, both it and the Virginians gave way completely. The tally: more than a hundred British lay dead or wounded, against three French dead and seventeen wounded. Bullets whistled, to be sure, but this time without nearly as much charm.[19]

The battle of Fort Necessity covered no one in glory. Still, Washington received official thanks for his efforts upon his return that autumn, and he labored to put the best possible construction on the whole sorry affair. Skeptics neverthe-less thought the young officer "imprudent," his field judgment "unmilitary," "too ambitious," even "infamous." Such criticism was not pervasive, in print at least, and scarcely unique to him. But it does invite us to step back a bit and remind ourselves that Washington's early career was in fact shaped as much by his own struggles as by those of his country. Preeminent historians, otherwise generous to his legacy, have observed that in these years Washington's shortcomings were not far to seek: Don Higginbotham notes that he was "too quick to blame others" and "exceedingly political" and concludes that "Washington's behavior was far from admirable." James Flexner summarized his subject's adventures in the Ohio thus: "militarily, Washington had shown both foolishness and ignorance." And John Alden: "He had offered fulsome and insincere flattery to British generals in vain attempts to win great favor. He had been youthfully arrogant. He had been jealous of competitors, tactless, and ungrateful."[20]

There is no need to belabor the point: Washington, like most young people, had a rough go of it in early adulthood. His struggle is distinctive and arouses interest because of the stage upon it was acted and the portents it carried for the coming time. By way of getting some perspective on this process, we will attend to a brief swatch of Washington's correspondence in the aftermath of his resignation from military service in late 1754 and prior to his volunteering as aide-de-camp to General Braddock, in early 1755. Here, between disappointment and aspiration, we discover Washington coming to understand, however fitfully, what honor can mean to him.

In October 1754 Governor Dinwiddie contemplated with some pleasure the riches before him. The Virginia Assembly and Commons had together released £40,000 to meet the public need. The money, along with a considerable stash of armaments, could not have come at a better time, and he quickly move to make the most of it. In concert with Governors Arthur Dobbs of North Carolina and Horatio Sharpe of Maryland, Dinwiddie set to work reorganizing the infrastruc-ture of his military forces. Heretofore regular and local companies operated within a vague and inefficient command structure, to the satisfaction of no one and to the intense irritation of the Governor above all. "As there have been some disputes between the regulars and the officers appointed by me," he explained to Halifax, "I am now determined to reduce our regiment into Independent Com-panies, so that from our forces there will be no other distinguished officer above a captain." Washington grasped immediately what this meant in personal terms: now a colonel, he would, under the new order of things, be reduced in rank and obliged to serve under those he had previously commanded.[21]

And so Washington resigned. He had every right to do so, of course, and for reasons familiar to military culture since time out of mind. Haggling over rank was virtually a constant in the eighteenth-century army; in due time, Washington himself would be driven nearly to distraction by such disputes. It is important to remind ourselves here of what lay behind these contests: not the colors so much, nor the money, really, but respect—ultimately, honor. As we have already noted, Washington came of age at a time and in a region where considerations of honor were the stuff of life—and sometimes death—itself. But to resign his commission for honor's sake does not mean that Washington fully understood what it meant to thus act; to put it another way, it does not indicate that he had arrived at the more fully developed and deepened sense of honor that would eventually ground his mature leadership. In the passages that follow, however fleetingly, we see glimpses that this process was nevertheless beginning, evidence too that Washington did not arrive on the scenes of public life prepossessed of those traits associated with honor. One did not claim honor as a form of entitlement; it was rather to be earned, usually the hard way.

Within a matter of weeks into his retirement, Washington received a letter from William Fitzhugh, a Maryland colonel representing the interests of Governor Sharpe, newly appointed Commander in Chief of the American army. Fitzhugh assured his correspondent that General Sharpe "has a very great regard for you, and will be every circumstance in his power make you very happy." For his part, Fitzhugh wrote, "I shall be extremely fond of your continuing in the service, and would advise you by no means to quit it." By way of encouragement, Colonel Fitzhugh suggested that perhaps arrangements could be made that, if not entirely satisfactory, might be enough to keep his friend commissioned in the officer corps at least. Washington's reply, written from Belvoir on November 15, falls rather short of the graciousness and generosity readers have come to expect of his later correspondence. It is in fact unabashedly self-regarding, defensive, and ill tempered.[22]

The letter's opening courtesies quickly give way to unasked-for explanations, for the most part devolving on the author's settled view that whatever the army had to offer, there remained disparities "too great to expect any real satisfaction or enjoyment on a Corps, where I once did, or thought I had a right to, command." As for the nominal commission: "This idea has filled me with surprise," Washington informed Fitzhugh, "for if you think me capable of holding a commission that has neither rank nor emolument annexed to it, you must entertain a very contemptible opinion of my weakness, and believe me to be more empty than the Commission itself." Having thus repaid Fitzhugh's efforts on his behalf, Washington proceeded to enumerate—to a fellow officer—the hardships and indignities that must attend returning to the field, not the least of which was that fact that he "Must be reduced to a very low Command, and subjected to that of many who have acted as my inferior Officers." Better, he sighed, to retire and tend to his ill health and fatigue "than subject myself to the same inconveniences, and run the risque of a second disappointment." After complaining of having been shabbily treated by Dinwiddie—a constant source of support and reward for the young officer—Washington concluded by announcing again the ultimate rationale for his resignation: "it was to obey the call of Honour, and the advice of my Friends, I declined it, and not to gratify any desire to leave the military line. My inclinations are strongly bent to arms."[23]

Washington's inclinations may have been bent toward arms, but the immaturity evident in these passages suggests that he had some thinking to do about where they would take him. Presumably he found time for reflection in the quiet of his Mount Vernon estate, where he had settled in for the deep winter. If he did, the young former colonel may have come to realize how blunt—how crude and self-serving—was the sense of honor with which he rationalized his decision to resign. For honor in this regard was registered in the negative, as a slight to his personal esteem and a threat to a reputation among friends. It was about honor as one hoped to receive it, something bestowed and burnished as a grant. Washington had not yet fully grasped its more positive meaning as a motive to action, a way of being and operating in the world in which one aspired not so much to receive honor but to act honorably, and that meant acting for and on behalf of others, for causes greater than oneself, greater than the pursuit of "rank or emoluments."

Washington needed a reason to grow beyond himself. And, as it often happened in his life, just such a reason presented itself in the form of a letter he received early in March 1755 from Robert Orme, a lieutenant in the Coldstream Guards. In the event, Orme was writing on behalf of General Edward Braddock, recently arrived in Virginia to take over planned operations for yet another expedition into the Ohio Country. The general had learned both of Washington's interests in the military way and also of the disputes checking those interests. Braddock, Orme wrote, had an offer sure to satisfy all parties: he would be "very glad of your company in his family [that is, as the general's aide-de-camp], by which all inconveniences of that kind will be obviated."[24]

Washington thought it a splendid idea: he would serve as a volunteer and thus rid himself of the vexations attendant on rank altogether. We need not make exaggerated claims as to the transformative effect this offer had on Washington, but there can be no missing the change in tone and content in his response to

Orme. The author still felt the need to mention the sacrifices that must be made and expenses borne; he still saw it as an opportunity to get a leg up in the profession of arms. But at least he said as much, admitted to being "a little biass'd by selfish and private views." More important, Washington was careful to state explicitly his motives for agreeing to the arrangement—a "desire I may have to serve, (with my poor abilities) my King and Country"—and expressed his gratitude to the general "for the favour he was kindly pleas'd to offer me." Later in April Washington similarly made it a point to assure John Robinson, Speaker of the Virginia House of Delegates, that his "sole motive" was "the laudable desire of servg. My Country; and not for the gratification of any lucrative ends." And to Carter Burwell: "I am just ready to embark a 2d. time in the Service of my Country; to merit whose regard and esteem, is the sole motive that induces me to make this Campaigne; for I can very truly say I have no views, either of profiting or rising in the Service, as I go a Volunteer, witht. rank or Pay, and am certain it is not in Genl. Braddock's power to give a Comm. That I wd accept."[25]

What can we learn from Washington's early experience in the field? The temptation to read backward from the record must be guarded against but is perhaps impossible to resist. At Newburgh, we will see at work a fully developed leader, utterly confident in his command and certain of his judgment of others. Leaving it at that, however, viewing the General as somehow sprung into the world wholly formed, is to reproduce the image so firmly fixed in the collective memory. In truth the young soldier struggled as most other young men do to negotiate the competing demands of self-interest and realities of which he was but dimly aware. If he did not always succeed in resolving these pressures on his convictions, he did give evidence of a capacity to do so. And, like some but not all young men, he showed these signs most clearly when put to the test: he seems to have grown most when placed in circumstances over which he could not entirely impose control. This much can certainly be said of Washington at this early stage: he proved himself consistently willing to place himself in just these circumstances, indeed aspired even at this young age to confront danger, to lead others, and so to lay just claim on the esteem of the world.

FORGING OF A PATRIOT

"During the tumultuous decades before weapons replaced words," observes Edmund Morgan, "Washington imbibed the ideas of republican liberty that animated the spokesmen for American independence. He cannot properly be counted as one of the spokesmen." This much is true, nearly. Washington in fact held office continuously from his first election to the House of Burgesses for Frederick County in 1758—later, for Fairfax County—until the outbreak of armed hostilities. To be sure, much of his early time in office was devoted to largely local affairs, and, aside from the usual frustrations with British mercantilist policies, Washington seemed content to benefit from his cordial relations with Governors Fauquier and Botetourt and to enjoy such social amenities as Williamsburg might afford during those relatively calm years before the storm. "He was happy to live in this manner," Flexner notes, "and he intended so to die."[26]

No such luck. The year of Washington's election as a representative for Fairfax County coincided with the passage of the Stamp Act, in 1765. Washington let his voice be heard as part of the widespread resistance to the Act and voted in support of the Burgesses' resolutions of protest. Still, as Alden stresses, his "language was cautious" and his efforts "not remarkably ardent." Washington was rather more exercised, it seems, by the similarly ill-fated Townshend Duties of 1767–69: together with his friend and neighbor George Mason, he helped compose the House's nonimportation agreement in April 1769. This statement Washington duly carried to Williamsburg the following month as a part of that body's petition for relief. Governor Botetourt would have none of it, of course, and dissolved the Assembly. Undeterred, its members retired to the nearby Raleigh Tavern and in short order adapted the resolutions of grievance. In no sense are we to interpret these activities as evidence of a radical sensibility at work—Washington was no Sam Adams and never would be. But he was allowing himself to be drawn into the colony's affairs and, more important, into colonial affairs generally. In the process, Washington was making his mark: not loudly, not with much color. But as the decade closed Washington had nevertheless established, in John Alden's words, "a reputation as the possessor of sound judgment, as a man of principle who could be trusted."[27]

The opening years of the new decade granted to Washington and his fellow colonists a breather of sorts. Boston, it was true, remained on edge in the aftermath of its "massacre" of March 5, 1770; for the most part, however, Washington was able to return to his beloved Mount Vernon, there to act the Virginia squire he most certainly was. A good life, by the standards of the day: busy with the management of the plantation and its enslaved Africans and with the social amusements and diversions to which his station entitled him. It did not last long. As if awakened from their collective slumber, Americans reacted with startling unanimity to the bundle of punitive acts passed in response to the tea affair of December 16, 1773. Early May accordingly found Washington back in Williamsburg attending the new session of the House of Burgesses, where sentiment against the closing of Boston harbor, among other stipulations of the "Coercive Acts," had grown to dangerous levels of intensity. Governor Dunmore, like his predecessor, obligingly dissolved the session and, once more, its members beat the well-trod path back to the Raleigh Tavern. There its leaders first floated the idea of an intercolonial assembly to formulate concerted plans for the defense of sovereign rights. To this end, Washington was chosen among several dozen others to gather on August 1, 1774, to nail down Virginia's position on the crisis. In the meantime, he, Mason, and perhaps several others were to compose a bill of particulars—a statement of grievances, principles, and plans—that would eventuate in the Fairfax Resolutions. These resolves, "the most far reaching and radical of any presented at the convention," Washington ushered through a meeting first at the Fairfax Courthouse on July 18 and ultimately to their adoption in Williamsburg on August 1. This much accomplished, Washington was in turn elected, along with Peyton Randolph, Richard Henry Lee, Patrick Henry, Richard Bland, Benjamin Harrison, and Edmond Randolph, to represent Virginia in Philadelphia the following September.[28]

Washington may have been, as James Flexner claimed, "at first unsuspicious of design, and then unwilling to enter into disputes with the mother country." No longer. The summer of 1774 proved a turning point in the Virginian's political consciousness, when quiescence gave way to the alarm over the events of the preceding year and the concerted resolve of his fellow colonialists. "I think the country never stood in more need of men of abilities and liberal sentiments than now," wrote Washington to his friend Bryan Fairfax, scion of the great Northern Neck family to whom he owed so much. Fairfax, though sympathetic to the frustrations of the planter elite, was deeply concerned with the direction the resistance was taking. To him Washington posted a series of letters beginning on July 4, 1774, and continuing until he took leave for Philadelphia in late August. From these letters we can glimpse Washington articulating for the first time a sustained perspective on the imperial crisis. There is nothing especially novel about the ideas he invoked; they are given neither elaborate exposition nor startling expression. But they are his own and as such grant us a vantage point from which to view the principles he believed mattered, the arguments he thought convincing, the actions he thought necessary.[29]

Washington was by nature a realist, and realists do not often yield to suspicion or fantasies of persecution. The steady beat of ministerial policy for the past decade, however, had at length forced Washington to confront what must seem to any rational mind less a matter of bungling than of outright conspiracy. He was scarcely among the first to think so, but neither was he the last. In any case, what had once lay hidden in the thicket of imperial rule could now be seen for what it was: a concerted design to subject the colonialists to a state of vassalage for England's own enrichment and in violation of every tenet of enlightened government. Among other things, this realization gave to Washington and to other

Americans a means to locate the source, intentions, and logic of their discontents. That is to say, it gave them the enemy.[30]

Every sign—the otherwise mystifying insistence on "virtual representation," the haughty refusal to even consider petitions of grievance, the quartering of troops—gave evidence of a plot against American liberties. "Does it not appear," Washington asked Fairfax, "as clear as the sun in its meridian brightness, that there is a regular, systematic plan for to fix the right and practice of taxation upon us?" The question was rhetorical, but time and again Washington would answer it in the same language, as if in repeating the message he would come ultimately to embrace its full range of implications. "Government," he insisted several weeks later, "is pursuing a regular plan at the expense of law and justice to overthrow our constitutional rights and liberties." Such fears were hardly groundless or speculative; indeed, the evidence was plain to see for those who cared to look. "What further proofs are wanted to satisfy one of the design of the ministry," asked Washington, "than their own acts, which are uniformly and plainly tending to the same point . . . to afix the right of taxation?"

Washington, like most unhappy colonists, understood that this issue of taxation—important in its own aspect—was but the entering wedge of a much greater set of threats to their liberty. This understanding had the effect of magnifying what might otherwise appear a relatively minor issue into a matter of the most profound importance. At stake seemed nothing less than what it meant to be an American. "I could wish, I own, that the dispute had been left to posterity to determine," confided Washington, "but the crisis is arrived when we must assert our rights, or submit to every imposition that can be heaped upon us, till custom and use shall make us as tame and abject slaves, as the blacks we rule over with such arbitrary sway."[31]

These are not the words of a frontier provincial. Washington's is the language of a man who is coming to see himself swept up in a confrontation of historical import, where principles lose their abstraction, lines are clearly drawn, and the imperative to act takes on the force of a moral command. James Flexner once commented that, while Washington was not given to intellectualizing a point, "the acceptance of a conclusion was taking an almost irrevocable step." Here we bear witness to Washington arriving at such a conclusion and bracing himself to take that step. He is becoming an agent in history; he can do no other. "Shall we," he asked, "whine and cry for relief, when we have already tried in vain? Or shall we supinely sit, and see one province after another fall prey to despotism?" The letters to Fairfax evince the unmistakable signs of a colonial coming to think of himself as something more than that—not yet the figure he will become, not yet a leader, but as one who speaks now in a different and far greater register. "I should much distrust my own judgment upon the occasion," he wrote, "if my nature did not recoil at the thought of submitting to measures, which I think subversive of everything that I ought to hold dear and valuable, and did I not find, at the same time, that the voice of mankind is with me."[32]

The voice is not yet entirely self-confident, the sentiments not yet revolutionary. They will be, soon enough, but for now we see Washington struggling to put into writing convictions earned in the face of an uncharted future. At a minimum, we find him expanding the reach of his moral imagination, thinking hard about the compulsive force of principles, bringing the enemy into his sights, and staking his claim to a ground he knows he must defend. For all the uncertainty, there is a measure of clarity afforded in the process: who is in the right, who in the wrong; which motives exalted, which base. As he prepared for the trip that would take him to Philadelphia and to scenes as yet unimagined, Washington paused to compose the last communication he would ever have with Fairfax, the companion of his youth. Reflecting on the recent train of events, Washington recalled that "an innate spirit of freedom first told me, that the measures are repugnant to every principles of natural justice; whilst much abler heads than my own hath fully convinced me, that it is not only repugnant to natural right, but subversive of the laws and constitutions of Great Britain itself, in the establishment of which some of the best blood in the kingdom hath been spilt." A few days later, Washington left for Philadelphia, a changed man.[33]

TRIALS OF FAITH

There the General kneels in prayer, his brightly colored uniform set off by the snow and wilds of the winter's encampment. He knows, we know, what is to come: the hunger and hardship, the despair that will surely try men's souls. Arnold Friberg's 1975 "Prayer at Valley Forge" captures, quietly, the lasting impression of that winter's ordeal, but its real power, however mythical, insists on something more than sheer abjection. Washington and the majestic horse beside which he bows are bathed in a golden swath of sunlight, a radiant promise that from the depths of suffering will come spring, as it must. Washington was not, as these things are typically reckoned, a religious man. But he was finely attuned to the springs of human nature and the spirit through which it is animated. Humanity, he understood, could bear only so much, but that was still a good deal, and, with due regard to the limits as well as the possibilities of that spirit, much could yet be demanded. It is a perilous matter, its success never certain. That Washington was able to ask and ultimately to receive so much from his men testifies to his capacity for grasping this key: that the movement from sacrifice to reward requires a rebirth of a kind, the ritual enactment of which we find staged on the fields of Valley Forge.[34]

We are at the outset confronted, yet again, with the ossifications of memory and myth. No real effort will be made here to clear it all away. They have their functions, and in any case historians can be quick to straighten us out about certain realities surrounding the encampment of 1777–78. Valley Forge was not remote, isolated, or ignored; the weather was not especially dire; and there was, after all, the camaraderie and stubborn pride native to life under such conditions. But other facts speak to different realities: thousands did in fact perish and more nearly, victims of disease and want; desertion was a constant threat; the supply system was crippled much of the time; and morale could and did plunge to dangerously low levels. For six months, Washington attended to the physical and spiritual need of more than ten thousand American troops. How he did so and to what effect will take us one more and final step on our journey to Newburgh.[35]

Late in December 1777 Washington and his army were pitched several days from their winter quarters some twenty miles from occupied Philadelphia. The events of the past several months and indeed the very choice of Valley Forge had proved complex and vexing. What, exactly, lay ahead no one could say, but the Commander in Chief was anxious to put the best face on the prospect before them. Within two days the army would settle in; for now, he wrote in General Orders for December 17, it was enough to give thanks for safe delivery and to assure his men "that by a spirited continuance of the measures necessary for our defence we shall finally obtain the end of our Warfare—Independence—Liberty and Peace." And they were not alone: France had been assisting the cause of America, and "Every motive," Washington declared, "irresistibly urges us—nay commands us, to a firm and manly perseverance in our opposition to our cruel oppressors—to slight difficulties—endure hardships, and contemn every danger." Congress having recently resolved on a day of thanksgiving the following day, "The General directs that the army remain in it's present quarters, and that the Chaplains perform divine service with their several Corps and brigades."[36]

Gratitude can be a difficult emotion to conjure up, much less sustain under certain circumstances, and the men may be excused if it did not come readily to mind. The very day broke grudgingly with little promise of brightening the hours ahead. Henry Dearborn confided to his journal that it was "Thanksgiving Day thro the whole Continent of America," but "god knows We have very Little to keep it with this being the third Day we have been without flouer of bread." As for gratitude, wrote Dearborn, "I think all we have to be thankful for is that we are alive & not in the Grave with many of our friends." Comfort of a kind, perhaps, but it too would come only with struggle and with the resolve born of Washington's "firm and manly perseverance." The army occupied the high ground of Valley Forge on December 19, there to begin the work of creating the small city that has featured so prominently in the American imagination ever since. For our purposes, the drama that was Valley Forge rewards one more visit, however brief, because it illustrates so well the qualities of mind and character that would serve Washington so effectively in the spring of 1783.[37]

In military contexts, abjection is above all a problem of morale, and this Washington understood in his very marrow. Without faith, such sacrifice as he demanded of his men is worse than nothing: it is betrayal. With it, sacrifice is made the fit object of honor and makes its own unique claim to the nation's thanksgiving. This transformation in turn requires a collective sense of rebirth, the shared conviction that mutual sacrifice makes possible new beginnings and new worlds. The Valley Forge experience teaches us that Washington appreciated the crucial role that ritual and its attending stagecraft can be made to play in this process, a forceful example of which we shall consider shortly.

Edmund Morgan has described George Washington as the "Aloof American," and so he was. In no sense, however, is this to be taken as a comment on the General's attachment to his men and their collective welfare. Washington's correspondence from Valley Forge provides us with unmistakable evidence to the contrary; he was in fact preoccupied with the wretched state of his army and never ceased badgering Congress for more provisions. Within a week after arrival he wrote to warn its president that "I am now convinced, beyond a doubt that unless some great and capital change suddenly takes place in that line, this Army must inevitably be reduced to one or the other of three things, Starve, dissolve, or disperse, in order to obtain subsistence in the best manner they can." By January he was confiding to Governor Patrick Henry of Virginia that "it is not easy to give you a just and accurate Idea of the Sufferings of the Troops at large. Were they to be minutely detailed," Washington wrote, "the relation so unexpected, so contrary to the common opinion of people distant from the Army, would scarcely be thought credible." February proved, if possible, even worse. "The present situation of the Army," Washington reported to Henry Champion, "is the most Melancholy that can be conceived." If sufficient supplies, especially cattle, could not be sent immediately, he despaired, then "with pain I speak the alarming truth, no human efforts can keep the Army from speedily disbanding."[38]

But of course the army did not disband. Many died, some left, and everyone complained. But it did not disband. To a degree this fact may be attributed to the professional status and pride of an army toughened by time and trial. "For so inestimable a jewel as the freedom of this Continent," wrote one soldier, "what fatigues, what toils, and what hardships ought we not to suffer? We ought to contemn every danger and despise every hardship." In part, too, we may ascribe such perseverance to the Herculean labors of Nathanael Greene, brought at length on board to rescue the quite nearly defunct supply system. And there was, to be sure, the miraculous appearance of one Lieutenant General Frederick William Augustus Henry Ferdinand Baron von Steuben. His pedigree was doubtful, his contributions evident for all to see. By April the weather was clearing, troops were reappearing in camp, and men reported on "a new spirit of discipline among the troops that is better than numbers. . . . You would be charmed," wrote one, "to see the regularity and exactness with which they march and perform their maneuvres." There was, finally, Washington himself, who, though beset by intrigue, second-guessing, and internecine quarrels, remained to his men the unmovable standard against which they and all others were to be judged. With the General among them, they declared, "All Hell couldn't prevail against us."[39]

For all this, Hell seemed reluctant to ease its grip on the upper hand. That was to change dramatically in the opening days of May, when Providence made itself known in the form of treaties of alliance and of commerce and amity with France. Rumors had been circulating virtually since Benjamin Franklin had been commissioned to work his wiles in Paris several years before. Now it was official—or nearly so (Congress would ratify the treaties on May 4), and Washington aimed to make the most of the opportunity. In doing so, he provides us with an opportunity to observe a master of stagecraft at work, a leader who grasps that rituals of celebration are hardly incidental to the imperatives of battle. Even among the hardened and scarred—*especially* among them—these rites serve as media of rebirth, when past suffering is given purpose and memory transformed into a confirmation of shared identity.

Washington was eager to act on the news but characteristically prudent. "I shall defer celebrating this happy event in a suitable manner," he promised Henry Laurens, "Untill I have liberty from Congress to announce it publically. I will only say, that the army are anxious to manifest their joy upon the occasion." Indeed it was, apparently so much so that the General allowed himself to go ahead with an unofficial announcement in General Orders: "The signal Instance of providential Goodness which we have experienced, and which have now almost crowned our labours with complete Success, demand from us in a peculiar manner the warmest returns of Gratitude and Piety to the Supreme Author of all Good." Thanksgiving so rendered, it was now time to ready the camp for the festivities of Wednesday, May 6. The grounds were to be spruced, the "necessaries" hidden from sight; promptness, discipline, and order were to be observed with strictest regularity; officers were to be held accountable for the comportment of their brigades, which were in turn to "vie with the other in arriving at the highest Pitch of Excellence."[40]

By Tuesday, May 5, Washington was at length able to declare the news he had waited for so long. "It having pleased the Almighty ruler of the Universe to defend the Cause of the United American-States and finally by raising up a powerful Friend among the Princes of the Earth to establish out liberty and Independence upon lasting foundations," he announced, "it becomes us to set apart a day for gratefully acknowledging the divine Goodness & celebrating the important Event which we owe to his benign Interposition." On the following day at 9 A.M. sharp, the troops assembled to hear the benediction and a reading of the treaties and after that enjoyed what Colonel Philip van Cortlandt was to recall as the "greatest day Ever yet Experienced in Our Independent World of Liberty." At 10:30 the battalions were armed and organized according to Washington's careful designs. After thirteen shots, a feu de joie and then: "Huzza!" "Long live the King of France!" Huzza!" "Long live the friendly European powers!" Huzza!" "To the American States!" Another round of thirteen, another rolling report, and the men were dismissed to their quarters for rum and revelry of a more informal kind. Washington and his officers retired to a feast of their own, where the General, noted young John Laurens, "received such proofs of the love and attachment of his officers as must have given him the most exquisite feelings."[41]

It was in all a splendid affair, "spent in mirth and rejoicing, and in very good order." Some had feared that the enemy might take advantage of the occasion for an opportune strike, worried that the "troops must have more than the common quantity of liquor and perhaps there will be some little drunkenness among them." Of that we may be sure, but no such threat was realized, and the day went off without a hitch and according to plan. One soldier recalled that he had never witnessed so "unfeigned and perfect joy as was discovered in every countenance." Washington himself could not have been more proud and told his men so: "The Commander in Chief takes particular Pleasure in Acquainting the Army," he declared in General Orders the following morning, "that their Conduct yesterday afforded him the highest Satisfaction; the Exactness and order with which their Movements were performed is a pleasing Evidence of the Progress they are making in military Improvement, and earnest of the pleasing Perfection to which they will shortly arrive, with a Continuance of that laudable Zeal and Emulation which so happily prevails."[42]

What are we to make of all this, if indeed anything? It would be possible, of course, to view the events of May 6 as a particularly elaborate variation on a pep talk. There is something to this: guns, rum, and music can together pick up one's spirits rather nicely. Such a view, however, requires that we discount the force of pageantry and the pride to which it gives expression among such men. Ritual, it scarcely needs to be said again, has always been central to the work of creating and sustaining military identity. The displays unfolding on the fields of Valley Forge that day give evidence that Washington grasped this truth, that he was in fact a master of martial psychology. A new campaign was coming; the enemy was bestirring itself; soon, quite soon, it would be time to move on and prosecute the battle to unseen ends. Those who would follow him into the future could do so only as they had been transformed by the Valley Forge experience. May 6 was their day to bear witness, in effect, to themselves before their leader, a means to collectively confirm and declare that such sacrifice as they had endured had forged anew their resolve. Thus readied, the army marched out of camp with a purpose greater than the sum of its hardships.

CHAPTER 2

Origins and Development of the Newburgh Crisis

"The army," warned George Washington "is a dangerous instrument to play with." No sane person has ever been known to argue this point, but we know that the temptation to do just that has haunted the benighted history of warfare since time out of mind. And in no circumstance is that temptation greater than during revolutionary moments, when ideals, desperation, and arms may conspire to regrettable effect. It is folly to imagine that the American revolutionists were, because of their republican convictions, somehow immune to such appeals. They too felt desperation, no less at the conclusion of the war than at its outset; though men of principle, they could not but contemplate the full range of means to their vaunted ends. Among those means was the use of the army to leverage the conduct of civil government, thus to play a most serious, a most dangerous game indeed. This chapter tells the story of how that game was played, why, and how it provided the enabling conditions for Washington's finest moment. At stake was nothing less than the age-old problem of subordinating military to political authority. Because that contest shows no signs of abating, the story remains as vital to the collective memory now as ever, and its lessons ought never to be allowed to fade. "The subordination and restraint of the Continental army," concludes Richard Kohn, "was one of the great legacies of the Revolution" and is still, "as it was in 1783, the sacred trust of the United States armed forces."[1]

The Newburgh crisis remains, in the words of its most careful student, "one of the most bizarre and little understood events in the history of the United States." It has thus persisted as an object of controversy, not least over the question of whether the events of March 1783 can even be plausibly labeled a "mutiny," a "conspiracy," or a "coup d'état." The full range and depth of details will probably never be recovered, and historians have offered up lively and competing versions of what actually happened and what interpretation is best placed on the episode. Few doubt its importance and implications for Washington's own legacy, the military establishment, constitutional law, and the prospects of republican government then and now. Still, the uncertainty and narrative complexity of events must impose certain limits on any version of the story that would eventuate in Washington's March 15 performance. Here seems the best point, then, to briefly register a few qualifications and to clear some ground for what follows.[2]

Any intrigue worthy of attention will wind its way deep into the thickets of past events, through any number of contingencies, personalities, and shaded recesses. The Newburgh affair is no different: the discontents that led to it may be traced well back to the origins of the war and indeed before. But we must start somewhere and at some time, and I have chosen to feature a relatively focused set of turning points bearing on the one issue that seems to have consistently demanded the attention and catalyzed the energies of Congress, the General, and the officers: the question, that is, of pay and, more specifically, of pensions. These turning points devolve on three related but distinct events: the provision of half pay for seven years in the spring of 1778; the provision of half pay for life in the fall of 1780; and the commutation of these lifetime pensions into a grant of full pay for five years in the spring of 1783. This is merely one way to proceed, of course, but it has the merit of fixing our attention on the career of a controversy that leads directly to the banks of the Hudson. There we will take up in some detail the final stages of the plot and attend in particular to the production and circulation of the two anonymous texts that ignited the long-simmering discontents of the officer class. A word, finally about a word: I have opted to use "crisis" as the best descriptor for what ultimately transpired on that day in the Temple. By doing so I mean not only to avoid terminological disputes but to underscore the sense of active judgment required at such moments of moral distress.[3]

The matter of pensions may not strike the modern student as an especially volatile issue. A moment's reflection, however, reminds us that by their very nature pensions cut to the heart of the social contract: in effect, the pension represents a kind of acknowledged debt owed to those who have invested their time, talent, and sometimes treasure for the good of the whole. How or whether a given company, institution, or nation-state chooses to make good on that debt can tell us a great deal about that institution's health and structural integrity. Little wonder, then, that so much recent unrest among public-sector unions and within the European Union is prompted by just such concerns. When an authorized body asks for individual sacrifice, it assumes a moral obligation to compensate the individual beyond the terms of his or her immediate responsibilities. Or does it? Are there some forms of enrollment that not only are free from pensioned obligations but explicitly repudiate the concept of long-standing debt altogether?[4]

A fair number of Americans—good patriots all—believed that some classes of the citizenry ought *not* in fact be compensated after their duty had been exercised. Among these, they claimed, was the officer class. Why not? Very broadly, the answer may be found in the ideological heritage handed down from the very nation against which the revolutionaries were pressing their cause. There is irony here, but it was well earned: from at least the days of Cromwell, English subjects had been alert to the manifold dangers presented by professional armies and those who rule over them. This view was not unchallenged, but it was bequeathed to American colonists in a kind of purified and principled stance against standing armies as such. A substantial literature attends to this collective suspicion, and no effort here will be made to provide a comprehensive review of that body. If we are to appreciate the intensity of sentiment mobilized against compensation for the officers, however, some attention must be paid at the outset to the question of standing armies.[5]

It was and remains a perennial problem and in many ways underwrites the basic theme of this book. What is the proper role relationship between a people and its army? By definition, the army represents a principle of force, of compulsion sanctioned by the will of the state and its leaders. To the extent that its function is to coerce by means of implied or actual violence, it may be thought to stand in direct opposition to the tenets of democratic or republican government. At the same time, such governments must, if they are to survive in a dangerous world, maintain a body capable of exercising martial force when necessary for the protection of the people's liberties and rights. An army among such people must therefore exist as a matter of trust—a tenuous, delicate faith liable to be shaken at any moment. The lessons of antiquity had taught the English to harbor this trust begrudgingly, for Caesars will come, and if not a Caesar, then a Cromwell. The upheavals of seventeenth-century England had only entrenched this suspicion of military bodies deeper into the collective memory, indeed made of those fears an article of faith in the lexicon of opposition writings ever since. So vexing was the issue that the settlement of 1688 inscribed in its charter protections against the despotic reach of standing armies, especially in but not limited to times of peace.[6]

Colonial patriots, themselves deeply if selectively read in the opposition writings of Harrington, Sidney, Trenchard, and Gordon, among other English Real Whigs, were in their turn keenly sensitive to the question thus posed. They understood, too, that it was not a matter of ideological abstractions or the subtleties of political theory. English colonialism and its wars of expansion in the late eighteenth century had inevitably implicated America in a vast and complex chess game of great power ambitions. Britain's triumph over France in the Seven Years War unquestionably played to the colonists' advantage on a number of fronts. But it came at a cost, not least the perceived need to retain British troops in their midst as protection against residual threats foreign and domestic. This presence was tolerated without undue trouble for most of decade after the conclusion of hostilities with France, if only because the troops were for the most part well behaved and well governed. The quartering of British soldiers in Boston in 1768 and the inevitable eruption of violence, which came on March 5, 1770, changed everything.[7]

"Unhappy was the invention of a standing army," wrote Lord Kames, "which, without being any strong bulwark against enemies, is a grievous burthen on the people." Why so? For Kames and scores of other critics of the institution, history answered that question with alarming certainty. Invariably, it seemed, standing armies "were raised under the specious pretence of defending the state." But discipline and subordination of the troops, all free men, proved impossible, and so, "in order to get soldiers more devoted, Princes were sensible that their armies ought to be composed of men, who having no property, no principle, might be ever as ready to march against their countrymen as against the enemy." Though a Briton, Kames wrote in language all too applicable to colonial fears. And if they needed more ammunition with which to contest their plight, English critics had plenty more to offer in this vein. Because standing armies must draw their fodder from the destitute and the mercenary, they could not help but pose a threat to the very society they were nominally designed to protect. Aside from "the Insecurity of our Liberties from a large Standing Army," Britannicus asked in 1758, "can we say our Properties are safe with them? Are our Laws such Locks as Swords and Bayonets cannot break? Have Standing Armies always been kept in Awe by Act of Parliament? Let us remember what a Standing Army did in Cromwell's Days, and reflect, that what hath been, may come again." A decade later, Pro Patria echoed the refrain: the very willingness of a people to countenance such armies, he suggested, was sorry proof of its waning virtue; however that may be, it was self-evident "that no Nation upon Earth ever did, or ever will, long preserve their Rights and Liberties, where large Standing Armies are maintained."[8]

American patriots had by the early 1770s crafted this anti-army rhetoric into a fine instrument of assault. The standing army, they understood, was at once deleterious on its own terms and deeply implicated in other tendencies. For one, it violated the constitutional order and represented an unlawful usurpation of a people's rights. This much John Hancock and friends declared before Thomas Hutchinson shortly after the Boston Massacre: "we have seen a standing army procured, posted and kept within this province, in a time of profound peace, not only without the consent of the people, but against the remonstrance of both Houses of Assembly! Such a Standing Army must be designed to subjugate the people to arbitrary measures. It is a most violent infraction of their natural and constitutional rights." Every March 5 until war's declaration, Bostonians were treated to bloody variations of the theme of the "massacre" and the role of standing armies, those agents of "corrupt and arbitrary power," in bringing it about.[9]

Professional armies, then, stood in direct violation of constituted rights of citizenry. That was a legal issue. Behind and in front of it was a second and the equally disturbing question of what such armies implied about the state of American virtue. A people worthy of freedom, the reasoning went, did not allow that freedom to be usurped by forces in their nature subversive of republican government. That was a moral issue. It went deep, and it still does. To condone a professional army in a time of peace—or even, thought some, in a time of war— was in effect to delegate responsibilities justly one's own. It was to hand one's musket to another and say, "Protect me. In turn I will help pay, feed, and house you." A dangerous bargain indeed, because it conceded that which was most precious, most necessary, for a free people: its virtue. Here was a lesson, wrote James Burgh, learned the hard way by "the common people of England," who, "having been long used to pay an army for fighting for them, had at this time for forgot all the military virtues of their ancestors."[10]

The question could not help but further trouble the meanings of virtue and "military virtue." How were they related? In what sense was it consistent with republican ideology to insist on competency in arms as a marker of citizenship? For proponents of citizen-in-arms and, in particular, the militia tradition, it made all the sense in the world. Standing armies, by arrogating to themselves those duties properly belonging to the citizenry, leave the people exposed not only to the depredations of that army, but to themselves. A kind of degeneracy sets in, in which this "Corruption of Manners will slide from one to another, till we are become universally despicable; the Consequence and Effect of the prevailing Notion, that our Army is solely to be relied upon, and that our Defence is nobody's Business, who is not paid for it." The militia, composed of free and propertied gentlemen, offered to displace the need for professional armies. Where the latter was mercenary (because paid), the former was local, invested, and loyal; the militia had something to fight for, and, because they fought for themselves, their families, their nation, and God, these home-grown forces could "take up arms to defend their liberties, with a design to lay them down as soon as the end proposed is obtained." A Carolinian writing during a stretch of martial law was understandably sharp in posing the alternatives facing all American in 1774: "Standing armies have enslaved the whole human race. It is much better with a well regulated militia to run the risque of a foreign invasion, than with a standing army to run the risque of slavery."[11]

Time and events would soon expose the limits of militia: they were and remain largely a fantasy, especially appealing for those fearful of control and blinded to the realities of modern warfare. But that does not make the image of an armed and virtuous citizenry any less potent, and it certainly remained vital at the end of the Revolution as a way of understanding and resisting the claims of the army and its officers. At this point, it is enough to let the always reliable Samuel Adams summarize the case against professional armies. The Newburgh crisis cannot be fully understood without taking seriously the kind of sentiments expressed here:

> A standing Army, however necessary it may be at some times, is always dangerous to the Liberties of the People. Soldiers are apt to consider themselves as a Body distinct from the rest of the Citizens. They have their Arms always in their hands. Their Rules and their Discipline is severe. They soon become attachd to their officers and disposd to yield implicit Obedience to their Commands. Such a Power should be watchd with a jealous Eye. I have a good Opinion of the principal officers of our Army. I esteem them as Patriots as well as Soldiers. But if this War continues, as it may for years yet to come, we know not who may succeed them. Men who have been long subject to military Laws and inured to military Customs and Habits, may lose the Spirit and Feeling of Citizens.[12]

Adams, as usual, distills the anxieties of his countrymen into their clearest and most potent form. Patriots well before the outbreak of armed hostilities had learned how to tap into these fears to decisive effect—and for good reason. Many colonists deeply resented the presence of an alien, professional, and seemingly mercenary force in their midst. Such armies were in the community but not of it, expensive, dangerous, subversive of civil norms, and withal a pestilence on the body politic.

Now, a fortiori, if so much could plausibly be claimed of standing armies, what of their officers? Like Adams, most patriots held them for the time being in high regard—they were for the most part good men in a just cause. But there seemed to be something in the nature of professional armies, in the power they wielded and its inevitable tendencies to excess, that threatened the republican prospect. These anxieties in turn prompted the long-standing insistence on militias as the preferred model of citizen soldiery, and, although events soon exposed the weaknesses of that model, the sentiments underlying it persisted.

The complaints which drew together the Newburg officers were scarcely novel. Since the very early phases of the war, efforts had been made to rectify what was widely but not universally considered to be the woeful undercompensation of the officer class. The fact that junior officers' pay was hardly distinguishable from that of the common soldier was notorious during the siege of Boston and thought to be the source of real mischief, if not actually debilitating to morale. It is of course the prerogative of military personnel of all classes to complain about pay; that is what soldiers do. But Washington and others understood only too well that the issue could lead to serious problems in recruitment, retention, and discipline. In short, the prospects of success, of winning the war, depended materially on such support as the country could solicit on behalf of those fighting for its existence. The struggle to meet these demands was checked, as usual, by the problem of supply. Ideological resistance to a professional officer class was thus complemented by straitened economic realities. The result was a frustrated and potentially dangerous admixture of resentment on all sides.[13]

By late 1777 the situation had become critical, and our story thus begins in that year at the encampment in White Marsh. Faced with the question of what the winter campaign might portend, Congress arranged in November to have a committee, composed of Robert Morris, Elbridge Gerry, and Joseph Jones, pay General Washington a visit. The aim was to learn of his plans, his needs, and the state of his army. In the event, they learned a great deal indeed, and reported back to Congress a frank and disturbing picture of life at camp. Washington had in the course of his discussions with the committee at headquarters made clear that a winter campaign under the circumstances would be ill advised in the extreme. The reasons were not far to seek, reported the committee, remarking with some alarm on "a general discontent in the Army and especially among the Officers." As far as Morris, Reed, and Gerry could tell, the distresses complained of were perfectly evident all around them, and so they promised quickly to lead Congress toward their remedy. In particular, the committee wrote, it hoped to "see the Military placed on such a footing as may make a Commission a desirable object to the Officer, and his rank preserved from degradation and contempt." To this end, the three men proposed a list of measures, headed by the recommendation "That an half pay establishment be formed and adopted in the American Service." The chain of events leading to Newburgh had forged its first link.[14]

In a letter of December 10, 1777, the committee at headquarters confided to Washington its hopes that "the prevailing discontents will subside." Their confidence proved illusory. The ensuing debates in Congress over the half-pay plan, noted Jonathan Trumbull Sr., rapidly surfaced as "the most painful and disagreeable question that hath ever been Agitated in Congress." Gouverneur Morris reported to the General that "no measure hath ever been more severely contested." Unable to get anything close to consensus on the matter, Congress at length appointed a new committee, composed of Horatio Gates, Thomas Mifflin, and Timothy Pickering, to pay yet another visit, this time to the rustic environs of Valley Forge. Again, the expedition proved illuminating. After consulting with Washington, the ambassadors put their report behind a resolution "that all military Officers commissioned by Congress, who . . . may be in the service of these United States, and shall continue therein to the end of this present War, shall . . . be entitled to receive annually, the one half of the pay of officers of equal rank in the actual service of the said United States."[15]

Washington was of course pleased with the direction of events, but cautiously so. He had been pressing for greater compensation for years; the dire circumstances at Valley Forge seemed now to provide a timely catalyst for some form of happy resolution. And so he pushed, and then he pushed some more. As the proposal for half pay reached its troubled resolution, Washington stressed to the president of Congress that "I do most religiously believe the salvation of the cause depends upon it, and without it, your Officers will moulder to nothing, or be composed of the low and illiterate men devoid of capacity for this, or any other business." Even granting the General's well-honed art of dunning Congress for more support, we cannot gainsay the very real sense of crisis that had descended on the army. "It will shake the very existence of the Army," Washington wrote fellow Virginian John Bannister, "unless a remedy is soon, very soon applied." Without half pay, he warned, the officers "will not be persuaded to sacrifice all views of public interest, and encounter the numerous vicissitudes of War, in the defence of their Country, unless she will be generous enough, on her part, to make a decent provision for their future support." Still the question remained unanswered: would the country, would Congress "be generous enough"?[16]

Not if Elbridge Gerry could help it. Like many of his fellow critics, Gerry, the proud Bay Stater, was convinced that "the infant state of the country, its aversion to placement and petitioners . . . the equality of officers and soldiers before the war" militated against the measure. Besides, the question itself was ill posed: at issue was not Americans' generosity—had they not been yielding their mite for going on half a decade now? The real question was whether provisions such as half pay were in truth consistent with the principles of republicanism and, more immediately, whether anything more could legitimately be asked of the oppressed taxpayer. If half pay stunk in the nostrils of men like Gerry, then it was for perfectly explicable historical, moral, and economic reasons. For James Lovell the whole thing seemed of a piece with European traditions, which threatened to introduce "into Society a set of haughty, idle, imperious Scandalizers of Industrious Citizens and Farmers." Henry Laurens, of all people, thought he detected in the plan a concession to aristocracy and a retreat from republican simplicity. He preferred to bank his fortunes on the "many Thousands whose hearts are warm with the seasonings which induced the original Compact and who have not bowed the Knee to Luxury nor to Mammon." From New Jersey, Abraham Clark dismissed the officers' complaints as rather too precious: "It is said many good officers are weary of the service, and wish to resign unless they are placed upon a permanent establishment. . . . Must we all therefore resign? This is no time to talk of ease and retirement. Let us first establish our liberties," Clark concluded, and "our desires of ease will then be obtained." These and many other counter-arguments were developed in more sophisticated ways in the years ahead, but even now they resonated with Americans without as well as within the walls of Congress.[17]

The answer to Washington's question, in any case, would not be forthcoming until well into the spring of 1778, and it came grudgingly at best. Representatives from Massachusetts, New Jersey, and South Carolina hotly contested the plan; supporters came mainly from the mid-Atlantic states and much of the South. By late March, Francis Lightfoot Lee, chairing, opened debate to a Committee of the Whole, from which was unleashed the "painful and disagreeable question" that could no longer be deferred. The first few days settled nothing. A month later, Congress drew a collective breath and waded into the battle once more. April 26 witnessed three pivotal votes: the first garnered support for half pay in principle; the second, on whether such pay ought to be limited in duration, failed; and the third, on a 6–5 count, recommended half pay for life. If there was joy among the victors, it did not last long. Opponents moved quickly to send the measure to the states for consideration there. Knowing full well that this would effectively kill it, supporters of half pay struck a compromise: half pay not for life but for seven years. The bill passed unanimously on May 15, 1778, and three days later Washington could announce in General Orders that officers "shall after the Conclusion of the War be entitled to receive annually for the term of seven years (if they live so long) one half of the present pay of such Officers." And so was the second link forged.[18]

To be an American, wrote Thomas Paine in the fall of 1780, was to contemplate "the undefaced remembrance of a lovely scene. To trace over in imagination the purity of the cause, the voluntary sacrifices made to support it, and all the turnings of the war in its defence, is at once both paying, and receiving respect." This was by any measure delusional. The year 1780 was if anything America's *annus miserabilis*, when on virtually every front the fortunes of war seemed most dismal, the prospects of nationhood most distant. Having resolved to dam the rivers of paper money flooding the country, Congress now faced the grim imperatives of retrenchment, administrative reorganization, and systemic reform of the army. To economic hardship was thus added the dispiriting news of major defeats in the southern theater, notably the losses at Camden and Charleston. Morale in

Congress, on the streets, at camp—especially at camp—was reaching dangerously low levels, and almost everyone knew it. Alexander Hamilton, nearly always a fair brake on romantic excesses, captured the reality in stark but necessary language: "Without speedy change the army must dissolve; it is now a mob, rather than an army, without cloathing, without pay, without provision, without morals, without discipline. We begin to hate the country for its neglect of us; the country begins to hate us for our oppression of them. . . . Held together by the slenderest of ties we are ripening for a dissolution."[19]

Not a promising context, then, for exacerbating the pay issue. Those who may have hoped that the steps taken in 1778 would resolve tensions over officer compensation were in quick order to be disappointed. Immediately after its passage, Washington had dared to believe that it would "quiet in a great measure, the uneasinesses which have been so extremely distressing, and prevent resignations which have proceeded to be at such a height, as to destroy our whole military system." It did nothing of the kind. The year was not even out before the General was forced to pick up the battle again, this time from the truly dire circumstances at Morris Town. It was a fact "too notorious," he told Joseph Reed, "that the Officers cannot live in the Army under the present circumstances. . . . These are severe tests of public virtue, and should not, in point of policy, be pushed too far." With the onset of a winter more distressing even than that at Valley Forge came the near collapse of the provisioning system and hence the inevitable threat of losing the officer corps. Many of them, Washington warned Benjamin Harrison, "from absolute necessity are quitting the Service and the more virtuous few rather than do this are sinking by sure degrees into begging and want."[20]

The Commander in Chief was not alone, of course, in voicing such fears. Soon enough—but just soon enough—there emerged from civilian ranks individuals with the resources, vision, and nerve to initiate major reforms across the board. The second phase of the half-pay and pension campaign unfolded within the context and as part of this more general overhaul. Leading the effort was the redoubtable figure of Robert Morris, whom we shall meet for more discussion later in the story. As the presiding financial genius in Congress and without, Morris had earlier floated the idea of enhancing the officers' compensation to include half pay for life; it went down quickly in the spring of 1779. But the idea hung on and was reanimated in the summer of the following year on the heels of an officers' memorial from the Fourth Regiment of Light Dragoons on August 3, 1780. Congress appointed a committee to look into the merits of the petition and duly received its recommendation to extend half pay for life. The ensuing deliberations yielded, among other assurances, the following resolution, which must have seemed choice to readers at camp: "That patience and self-denial, fortitude and perseverance, and the cheerful sacrifice of time, health and fortune, are necessary virtues which both the citizen and soldier are called to exercise, while struggling for the liberties of their country; and that moderation, frugality and temperance, must be among the chief supports, as well as the brightest ornaments, of that kind of civil government which is wisely instituted by the several states in this union." As for the motion: it failed, although Congress did manage to conjure up the promise, if not the means, to provide a pay raise for the men, staff, and officers.[21]

The news was disappointing, but momentum played to the "nationalists," for whom the pay measure was part of an intricate plan of reform and renewal. Nothing if not resourceful, these actors, among them the Morrises and Hamilton, set out to garner as much support as possible. They found it, most importantly from their General, who could be counted again to buttress the case. On August 20, 1780, he wrote from Orange Town to Congress a long and plaintive letter bearing directly on the matter of support for the army generally and for the officers in particular. The missive is important for its timing, its clearly rhetorical ambitions to alarm and motivate, and its explicit endorsement of half pay for life. If something was not done, and soon, Washington warned, the army "must either cease to exist at the end of the Campaign, or it will exhibit an example of more virtue, fortitude, self-denial, and perseverance than has perhaps ever yet been paralleled in the history of human enthusiasm." The half-pay-for-life idea, he thought, would go a long way toward deflecting the evils that must attend such want. Pennsylvania's willingness to provide just such support was evidence that it could be done, but, left to that state or any other, such a plan must set in embarrassing relief the failure of others to provide for the men. The remedy was, for Washington, self-evident, and it was a cure only the federated Congress could deliver: "I have often said, and I beg leave to repeat it," wrote Washington, "the half pay provision is, in my opinion the most politic and effectual that can be adopted."[22]

At length the newly energized Congress bestirred itself to pass a set of major initiatives, including provision for orphans, children, and widows and reorganization of executive departments. On October 21, it resolved in the affirmative "That the officers who shall continue in the service to the end of the war, shall be also entitled to half pay during life, to commence from the time of their reduction." It did not bode well that every vote cast against the measure came from New England states; indeed, Benjamin Huntington recalled, "Every Possible argument against the Measure was Adduced by its Opponents but to no purpose." As for Washington, he was happy to rehearse his long-standing conviction that the measure was "the most economical, the most politic, and the most effectual that could be devised," certain that as a result "the officers would be tied to the Service, and would submit to many momentary privations, and to the inconveniences, which the situation of public affairs makes unavoidable." Hamilton, not surprisingly, was of one mind with his boss: "The placing of officers upon half pay during life," he wrote afterward, would prove to be "a great stroke of policy, and would give Congress a stronger tie upon them, than anything else they can do."[23]

That much, for its critics, was exactly the measure's basic problem. Half pay for life was but one additional means of consolidating loyalties within a superintending body, concentrating power at the center at the cost of state sovereignty and, ultimately, republican virtue itself. Again James Lovell pounced: to John Adams he complained that "we had once an Army fighting for Republicans but they say they are now fighting the battles of asiatic speculators." This kind of largess seemed to many to come at the worst possible time and so gave "inexpressible pain" to Abraham Clarke, who nevertheless gave full expression to his resentments at seeing "Congress Sporting away the publick money and increasing debt at the very time we are in a Perfect State of bankruptcy." Samuel Huntington was more measured but no less adamant: he was quite willing to reward the officers and appreciated their contributions to the cause but avowed himself to have "ever been opposed to Pensions for Life as a reward for their Services, as inconsistent with the Genius and Spirit of our Constitution." The officers, the nationalists, and Washington had nevertheless prevailed against the tides of resistance. But, like the war, their battle was far from over.[24]

Passage of half pay for life represented victory, but victory of a kind only. The officers, indeed Americans generally, had long since come to learn the difference between a promise and its delivery. The fact that the measure was produced toward the end of 1780 could not have done a great deal to buoy the army's spirits in any case. Although we have noted in passing the woes besetting the revolutionary cause, it might be well to remind ourselves again of just what the aspirants were dealing with: in fact or in perception, they were looking at pervasive war fatigue among their fellow patriots, growing skepticism about the claims of the army and its officer corps on the commonwealth, a financial system in near collapse, refractory states bent on scaling down expenditures across the board, alarming defeats on southern battlefields, Arnold's treason, mutiny in the state lines, and a Congress riven by internecine strife. Little wonder, then, that the extension of half pay for life failed, despite Washington's hopes, to quiet the men, much less inspirit an officer class that knew a mess when it saw one.[25]

Skepticism is not the same as defeatism, however, and forces were evidently at work to resolve both the acute and the chronic ills besetting the would-be republic. For several years a small but enterprising group of "nationalists" had been angling to figure out ways of rectifying the situation, and, while they frequently met defeat, this cadre of reformers was fast bringing its program into sharper focus. Among them were Philip Schuyler, James Duane, Gouverneur Morris, and Alexander Hamilton. They were, as Carp succinctly puts it, "an abrasive, individualistic group, united less by their economic status or social position than by their contempt for Congress; important and lethargic management of the war and by their conviction that its powers had to be strengthened if the war was to be won." Intellectually, Hamilton stood out from the beginning as its most articulate—and tireless—voice. In September 1780 he arrived at what would become the key strategy driving the nationalists' campaign: "two things let me recommend," he wrote Duane, "as fundamental rules for the conduct of Congress—to attach the Army to them by every motive" and, in the process, "maintain an air of authority (not domineering) in all their measures with the states. The manner in which a thing is done has more influence than is commonly imagined." Secure the loyalty of the army and establish the preeminence of Congress: here were the means. And the ends? Winning the war, of course, and establishing the soundest possible foundations for an independent, credible, and lasting republic.[26]

None of this was viable, however, without the money to make it so. Here was the gist of the problem, and the nationalists took it as their first, only, and ultimate goal to find the financial resources sufficient to victory and the launch of nationhood. At its heart, explains Jack Rakove, the nationalist program was clear, if not so simple of execution: "restoration of public debt on a permanent foundation, predicated on the establishment of a recognized national debt, to be serviced by Congress through the allocation of specific revenues to its treasury." Only one man, fair to say, could boast the talents necessary to conceive and deliver on the plan to overhaul the system, and Congress found him in the person of Robert Morris. The former Pennsylvania representative and merchant prince in time became, as Merrill Jensen observes, "the all-powerful force in every department, in Congress, in the army, and wielded more power in the United States than any man had yet done." It was not so much his individual talents—a head for numbers, experience, and dedication to the cause—that recommended Morris so compellingly. Others might reveal similar qualities. It was rather the degree, intensity, and magnitude of his gifts that secured his appointment as Superintendent of the newly created Department of Finance and, indeed, his claim to posterity. Like Hamilton, who would in time supplant his older friend as the nation's presiding financial genius, Morris aimed "to unite the several states more closely together in one general money connection and indissolubly to attach many powerful individuals to the cause of our country by the strong principle of self-love and the immediate sense of private interest."[27]

In the course of securing these ends, Morris invited his share of controversy, scandal, resentment, and sometimes fear. He could be imperious and impatient, susceptible, if not always fairly, to charges of favoritism and of being rather too solicitous of his own "private interest." No one, however, doubted his financial acumen or commitment to the cause. And while Rakove properly warns against overstating his role as a "party" leader of the nationalists, he seldom hesitated to put himself in front or in the middle of virtually all the major financial initiatives of the time. He did not always succeed, of course: his much-vaunted effort to pass a 5 percent impost and several other revenue-generating schemes ultimately met defeat at the hands of the states and opponents in Congress. But, as we might say today, the man knew how to play hardball, and these reversals merely provoked Morris and his supporters to more aggressive, more daring strategies. When Congress took up again the bundle of pay issues in the summer of 1782, Morris, Hamilton, Gouverneur Morris, and their cohort were thus primed to take their mission in a new direction. What they needed above all was muscle from without the doors of Congress, muscle strong enough that, when it was flexed, the people could not help but notice and—perhaps—recoil in fear.[28]

The offensive found its opening late in 1782. With peace impending, Morris found his appeals for permanent revenues as a means to aid the war effort of limited effect. His hopes for the impost dashed by the stubborn localism of Rhode Island and Virginia, Morris banked his all on securing the aid of first public creditors and then the army, both of which, he argued, must be appeased if the nation was to command the trust and credibility of Americans at home and potential friends abroad. The public creditors—private parties from whom Congress had been borrowing money for years—could relatively easily be brought into the game. More challenging—much more—would be the army, which, though disgruntled, could not be assumed willing partners in the plan now unfolding. Still, the opportunity proved too enticing, and arrangements were made to capitalize on its discontents. And so, as Rakove puts it, "Rather than scale down his program to the emerging though auspicious realities of 1783, Morris committed himself to manufacturing a crisis that he hoped would alarm Congress into adopting his scheme of public finance."[29]

As chance would have it, a delegation had arrived in Philadelphia after Christmas 1782 bearing the nationalists a most precious gift. General Alexander McDougall, Colonel John Brooks, and Colonel Mathias Ogden had traveled from the grounds of Newburgh intent on an appointment with Congress. To it they would submit a memorial from the officers detailing their accumulative grievances, requests, and hopes for resolution of their pecuniary interests. The "Address and Petition of the Officers of the Army of the United States" was not altogether a surprise: Benjamin Lincoln and Arthur St. Clair had been assiduously priming its reception in the city for weeks. Drafted by Henry Knox after he led a more local—and doomed—effort before the Massachusetts authorities, the memorial offers us a perfect distillation of the officers' complaints and state of mind on the threshold of the crisis.

Stout Henry Knox, bookish and amiable, had long shown himself to be a man worth taking seriously. In September 1782, leaders of the Massachusetts line had tested the waters by sending a delegation to Boston, where a list of grievances was submitted for consideration before the General Court. Finding no recourse there, the officers in November quite naturally turned to the sympathetic Knox and secured his assistance in the composition of a memorial; a draft was vetted to the lines at Newburgh and then placed in the hand of McDougall, Brooks, and Ogden. Washington, let it be said, was well aware of the proceedings, indeed helped prepare for its ultimate reception in Philadelphia by stressing to his contacts there the dire state of affairs and the army's agitated frame of mind. A week into the new year, Congress received the memorial. By their nature, such petitions require a degree of deference, but, far from cringing before "the supreme power of the United States," the memorialists laid out with unmistakable clarity the basis of their concerns. "We have struggled with our difficulties year after year," declared the officers, "under the hopes that each would be the last, but we have been disappointed. We find our embarrassments thicken so fast and have become so complex, that many of us are unable to go further." Such measures of pay that had been addressed in the past, they pointed out, had been swallowed by inflation and middlemen; "Our difficulties are brought to a point. We have borne all that we can bear, our property expended—our private resources are at an end—and our friends are wearied out and disgusted with our incessant applications." Accounts remained outstanding, provisions undelivered, with little hope for relief under the current system of pay.[30]

By way of solution, the Newburg delegation offered up a plan of its own. The half-pay pension resolution passed in 1780 was in itself "an honorable and just recompense for several years hard service, in which the health and fortunes of the officers have been worn down and exhausted." Mindful, however, of public sentiment against coddling an officer corps past its term of active service, the petitioners proposed a compromise of sorts: "to commute the half-pay pledged, for full pay for a certain number of years, or for a sum in gross, as shall be agreed on by the Committee sent with this address." A lump sum, then, paid in full at an appointed time: this much seemed only fair and certainly reasonable under the circumstances. The memorial professed its faith that Congress would attend to the matter in earnest but sharpened the edge of its case by reminding members that "It would be criminal in the officers to conceal the general dissatisfaction which prevails, and is gaining ground in the army, from the pressure of evils and injuries, which, in the course of seven long years, have made their condition, in many instances, wretched. They therefore entreat that Congress (to convince the army and the world, that the independence of America shall not be placed on the ruin of any particular class of citizens) will point out a mode for immediate redress."[31]

Shortly after receiving the memorial, Congress appointed a Grand Committee composed of one delegate from each state. Its charge was to contemplate the general state of affairs in the army, in particular questions of past, present, and future pay and settlement of material accounts. Any such discussion would have to lead first to Morris, the government's financier, and to his office the Grand Committee soon repaired. To the surprise, presumably, of absolutely no one, Morris protested that while he would be only too happy to help, there was simply no way he could do so under the current revenue arrangements. At this point, Morris had resolved himself into a state of habitual exasperation, which, like most chronic conditions, seemed only to deepen with time. "Imagine the Situation of a Man who is to direct the Finances of a Country," he confided in Franklin, "almost without Revenue. . . . An Army ready to disband or Mutiny, A Government whose sole Authority consists in the Power of framing Recommendations." Pressing forward, on January 13 the Grand Committee next called before it the Newburgh delegation of officers, whereupon members were treated to another round of lamentation and scarcely veiled threats of mutiny. As Morris continued to capitalize on these frustrations, Congress arranged for a subcommittee composed of James Madison, John Rutledge, and Samuel Osgood to meet with the appropriate parties. The subcommittee submitted its report on January 22.[32]

The ensuing debate was soon interrupted by the bombshell news of Morris's announcement that he intended to resign his office as Superintendent of Finance. His intentions to do so were undeniably complex—and justified—but it is likely that he was both sincere in tendering his resignation and seeking to add a heightened sense of urgency to the situation. In any case, Congress resolved on January 25 to act on the subcommittee's proposals. Morris was granted discretionary powers to deal with matters of present pay and to settle the army's past accounts with the assistance of the states. As for the half-pay issue: after debate over its duration, the proposal twice went up for a vote; twice it went down to defeat. On February 4 its supporters tried again: twice up, twice down. The time had come for strategy of an altogether different kind.[33]

The Newburgh delegation had been directed to keep Knox and his men apprised of their efforts in Philadelphia. On February 8, accordingly, Colonel Brooks returned to camp with several letters. The first, written by McDougall and Ogden, told of their labors and of the meager results obtained: a month's pay in notes for the officers and men, to be distributed in weekly installments. The half-pay question commutation was, regrettably, deferred for another day, when presumably the option of going to the states would be settled. This was a sticking point: even if the states were inclined to fund commutation, which was doubtful, the campaign for continental assumption of the debt would be thereby checked. For this reason, Knox's correspondents explained, "some of our best friends in Congress declared, however desirous they were to have our accounts settled and the commutation fixed, as well as to get funds, yet they would oppose referring us to the states for a settlement, till all prospect of obtaining continental funds was at an end."[34]

The second letter, from Gouverneur Morris, was for Knox's eyes only, and for good reason. The author was a very bright man, of unquestioned allegiances and solid republican credentials. But he was not an especially subtle man. As part of the inner circle conspiring to "manufacture" the crisis rapidly unfolding, Gouverneur Morris sought now to reel in Washington's camp favorite. "It has given me much Pain," he confessed to Knox, "to see the Army looking wildly for a Redress of Grievances to their particular States." It was folly, Morris argued, to expect support where none had been forthcoming; now, with peace on the horizon, the states had even less incentive to open up their purses. "During the War they find you useful and after a Peace they will wish to get rid of you and then will see you starve rather than pay a six Penny Tax." The army need not put itself into a position, however, if its leadership rightly understood and acted upon the plan at work: "The Army may now influence the Legislatures," Morris hinted, "and if you will permit me a Metaphor from your own Profession After you have carried the Post the public Creditors will garrison it for you." The financier had said much the same thing: "if the Army can be kept together in a respectable Situation," Robert Morris had written, "their Influence (joined to that of the other Public Creditors) will probably obtain Funds for the Public Debts." But Gouverneur Morris was not speculating: he was making a proposal, and flirting with mutiny at the same time. Knox would have none of it. Alarmed by Morris's intimations, he insisted to McDougall that his men would instead "suffer wrongs and injuries to the utmost verge of toleration rather than sully it in the least degree."[35]

If Knox could not be seduced, might the General himself? The thought is in retrospect absurd on its face, but at the time the prospect must have proved enticing. There was in any case no chance whatsoever of things moving forward without plotting Washington's role in the scheme afoot. What would be that role? The Commander in Chief had been thus far relatively quiet on the events unfolding, although he surely knew of their general direction. His fondest hope at this time, he wrote General Heath, was to quit "these rugged and dreary

Mountains" and return to the vines and fig leaves of Mount Vernon. Otherwise, Washington was occupied with the routine rhythms of camp life, including the vexations of supply and discipline. Although his chaplains were alarmingly hard to come by of late, Washington thought the "New building" near enough completion to host weekly spiritual services. No harm and much good, he reasoned, might come from the "public Homage and adoration which are due to the supreme being, who had through his infinite goodness brought our public Calamities and dangers (in all humane probability) very near to a happy conclusion." Not just yet, however.[36]

Only one man blended within himself the requisite strains of intelligence, audacity, and stealth to handle the Washington question. Alexander Hamilton had served as his chief's aide-de-camp earlier in the war and had sustained more or less positive relations with him throughout. The New Yorker's indefatigable energies in Congress were bent fully toward the realization of the nationalist program: no one save Robert Morris worked as tirelessly on its behalf. Defeats on the floor seemed only to spur Hamilton to greater exertions. All now depended upon restoration of public credit, federal assumption of the debt, and the grounding of the new nation upon a sound economic basis. To this end he needed in his corner the army, its officers, and its Commander in Chief. Without the latter: nothing.

As communications between Philadelphia and Newburgh heated up, Hamilton gathered his thoughts and wrote a remarkable letter to Washington on February 13. "The state of our finances was perhaps never more critical," he wrote, and he was now "certain that there has scarcely been a period of the revolution which called for more wisdom and decision in Congress." Those being in regrettably short supply, the grievances of the army would remain unaddressed for the foreseeable future. But the situation was not hopeless: "The claims of the army urged with moderation, but with firmness, may operate on those weak minds which are influenced by their apprehensions more than their judgments." The army, that is, might secure satisfaction by letting it be known that it would not play the victim. Asserting itself on behalf of itself, the army would thus "add weight to the applications of Congress to the several states." The problem, then, was not in rousing the army's wrath; that much was given. The real difficulty, Hamilton observed pointedly, "will be to keep a *complaining* and *suffering army* within the bounds of moderation." And the solution to that difficulty, of course, was and only could be Washington. His influence was crucial to so managing the position of the army as to let its power be felt but not so much as to lose control over it. The key was that Washington's hand in all this not be evident: "it is of moment to the public tranquility," warned Hamilton, "that your Excellency should preserve the confidence of the army without losing that of the people. This will enable you in case of extremity to guide the torrent, and bring order perhaps even good, out of confusion. Tis a part that requires address; but 'tis one which your own situation as well as the welfare of the community points out."[37]

This is extraordinary counsel. Aside from the sheer nerve on display, Hamilton's letter is a masterpiece of insinuation, coyness, and brinksmanship. It is also deeply cynical, coldly calculating, and blithe: the author has no doubt, no misgivings, over a concerted design to use the country's military as an instrument for political ends. This not to say that Hamilton was oblivious to or dismissive of the army's genuine complaints; it is to stress the lengths to which he would apparently go to realize his ambitions. Washington knew his young adviser well, however, and in time responded with some counsel of his own. He need not be told how stressed were circumstances among his officers and army; nor would the straitened state of the country's finances come as news. The General was most disturbed, rather, by being fixed in a seemingly impossible bind. "The predicament in which I stand as Citizen and Soldier," wrote Washington, "is as critical and delicate as can well be conceived. The sufferings of a complaining Army on one hand, and the inability of Congress and the tardiness of the States on the other, are the forebodings of evil, and may be productive of events which are more to be deprecated than prevented." By nature and necessity an optimist, Washington nevertheless held out the hope that reason would prevail. He would in any case "pursue the same steady line of conduct which has governed me hitherto; fully convinced that the sensible, and discerning part of the Army, cannot be unacquainted (altho' I never took pains to inform them) of the Services I have rendered it on more occasions that one." Besides, Washington confidently predicted, the states would finally come around. Surely they could not "be so devoid of common sense, common honesty, and common policy as to refuse their aid on a full, clear, and candid representation of facts from Congress."[38]

James Madison was not so sure. By late February, the young Virginia delegate reported to his journals that events seemed to be coming together in ominous ways. On the 20th he reported Hamilton and Hugh Peters as declaring it certain "that the army had secretly determined not to lay down their arms until due provision and a satisfactory prospect should be afforded on the subject of their pay." Five days later, Madison confirmed the rumor if not the fact: "The discontents and designs of the army are every day taking a more solemn form," he wrote. "It is now whispered that they have not only resolved not to lay down their arms till justice shall be done them but that to prevent surprize a public declaration will be made to that effect." The grounds were being well plotted, apparently, and bearing the hoped-for harvest of rumor, anxiety, and a keen sense of impending danger.[39]

On March 8 Colonel Walter Stewart, a trusted ally of the Philadelphians (and Washington's Inspector General for the Northern Department), was directed to the cantonment on the Hudson, thence to Horatio Gates's headquarters. What exactly transpired between them must be a matter of speculation; indeed, Gates's own role in the planning and execution of the Newburgh plan has been the object of some dispute. On the one hand, as we have noted, Gates had had a rough go of it since the glories of Saratoga; Washington had had him yanked out of the South after Camden in 1780, and Gates had not stopped complaining about it since. On the other hand, Gates had proved beyond question his American loyalties, had consented to serve as Washington's second-in-command at Newburgh, and was, after all, tired, perhaps beaten. It thus must remain unclear just what he really had to gain from fomenting discord of this kind. But there he was, the presiding officer of a cabal bent on inciting at best mischief of an unwonted sort, at worst an outright coup d'état.[40]

What is certain is that at some point Gates and his supporters enlisted the rhetorical talents of Captain John Armstrong Jr. (1758–1843). Son of a prominent brigadier general with considerable experience of his own, Armstrong had been at Gates's side since early in the war; he would eventually serve (unhappily) as Secretary of War under Madison and then retire to a life of writing and pastoral pursuits. The decision to employ Armstrong was a good one: as his productions would demonstrate in very short order, he could write with energy, precision, and authority—that is, with a command of the language such as any military man might respect. On Monday, March 10, there issued from Gates's headquarters two communications, which rapidly made their way through camp and into the hands of the intended audiences. The first was a brief announcement, a call for a meeting to be held the next day at 11:00 A.M. in the Temple. "A commissioned officer from each company is expected," the note read, "and a delegate from the medical staff. The object of this convention is to consider the late letter [Brooks's of February 8] from our representatives in Philadelphia, and what measures (if any) should be adopted to obtain that redress of grievances which they seem to have solicited in vain." Clear enough: but the signs were not good from the outset. No one possessed the authority to call such a meeting but the Commander in Chief, and the letter's anonymity spelled trouble ahead.[41]

Shortly thereafter, a second, much longer address was sent on its way. None but the invested parties knew of its author at the time, but all were treated to a tightly composed, indeed eloquent appeal designed specifically to rally the officers prior to Tuesday's scheduled meeting. It repays close attention. The author labors early to make clear that he is one of them and that, like his fellow officers, he is operating from principle and from a sincere commitment to a glorious cause. His patriotism is not to be questioned: "he has long shared in your toils, and mingled in your dangers,—he has felt the cold hand of poverty, without a murmur, and has seen immolence of wealth, without a sigh." He had hoped only for victory over the enemy and that now, with that prospect so close, his faith and his republican virtue might be rewarded by those who have benefited from his sacrifice. "He hoped that as the clouds of adversity scattered, and as the sunshine of peace and better fortune broke in upon us,—the coolness and severity of government would relax, and that more than justice, that gratitude, would blaze forth upon those hands, which had upheld her, in the darkest stages of her passage, from impending servitude, to acknowledge independence." Alas, recent events and news from Philadelphia had put the lie to such hopes, and now the officers were confronted with the option of either supinely accepting the injustices to which they were being subjected or acting as men on their own behalf.[42]

The officers had given their all, and now peace offers its bounty. But upon whom, the writer asks, would it fall? "A country willing to redress your wrongs, cherish your worth, and reward your services?—A country courting your return to private life, with tears of gratitude and smiles of admiration? . . . Or is it rather a country that tramples upon your rights, disdains your cries, and insults your distresses?" The rhetorical questions mount, the indictments heaped one upon the other, the staccato pacing of the prose mirroring the sense of emergency it would impart. The officers had exhausted conventional means of seeking redress, the slow, servile, pointless process of petition and plea. Action of an altogether different order was now demanded. Otherwise, the men must resign themselves to complicity in their own subjection. There remained no middle ground, and the only real question now was:

> Can you then consent to be the only sufferers by this revolution,—and retiring from the field, grow old in poverty, wretchedness and contempt?— Can you consent to wade through the vile mire of dependency, and owe the miserable remnant of that life to charity, which has hitherto been spent in honor?—If you can—Go—and carry with you the jest of Tories, and the scorn of Whigs—the ridicule, and what is worse—the pity of the world.—Go—starve and be forgotten.[43]

The alternative was plain to see, the means at hand and the ends entirely principled. Resolve to make yourselves heard, the author advises; abandon the petition as worse than useless; gather together men of literary talent and lay out your remonstrance in the strongest possible language—the sacrifices, the faith, the perseverance, the disappointments and humiliations. And when you have done that, when you have demonstrated beyond question your commitment and your exasperations, then turn to your civilian leaders and lay down the terms of your satisfaction. Tell them, he urges, that

> although despair itself can never drive you into dishonor, it may drive you from the field—That the wound often irrigated and never healed, may at length become incurable,—and that the slightest mark of indignity from Congress now, must operate like the grave, and part you forever. That in any political event, the army had its alternative.—If peace, that nothing shall separate you from your arms but death.—If war, that courting the auspices, and inviting the direction of your illustrious leader, you will retire to some yet unsettled country, smile in your turn, "and mock when their fear cometh on."

Let it be said, too, concludes the address, that the officers hoped it would not come to this, that they would be only too happy, in finding satisfaction, to "withdraw into the shade of private life, and to give the world another subject of wonder and applause—and army victorious over its enemies—victorious over itself."[44]

Washington was in due course apprised of the texts circulating through camp. If he was alarmed, he did not show it. In all likelihood, he suspected that something along these lines was in the offing, though uncertain as to the timing and the specific form. But he did move quickly: on the morning of Tuesday, March 11, he countermanded the call for a meeting in the day's General Orders as a deviation from regular procedure. As a measure of his good faith, concern for the men, and confidence in their professional judgment, Washington opted instead to call "the General and Field officers with one officer from each company and a proper representative of the staff of the Army" at noon in the Temple on Saturday the 15th. After then discussing the matter and deciding "what further measures ought to be adopted as most rational and best calculated to attain the just and important objects in view," the senior officer [Gates] "will be pleased to preside and report the result of the Deliberations to the Commander in Chief." Apparently, Washington was not to be on the scene of the meeting itself.[45]

On Wednesday, March 12, Washington composed a letter to Congress informing it of his "inexpressible concern" regarding the proceedings of the previous several days. Including copies of the announcement and address, the General stated simply his hope that "the measures I have taken to dissipate a Storm, which had gathered so suddenly and unexpectedly, may be acceptable to Congress" and promised to "continue my utmost Exertions to promote the wellfare of my Country under the most lively Expectation, that Congress have the best Intentions of doing ample Justice to the Army, as soon as Circumstances will possibly admit." How sudden and unexpected were these circumstances is unclear. Two week earlier Washington had heard from Joseph Jones of rumors in Philadelphia "that here are dangerous combinations in the Army, and within a few day past it has been said, that they are about to declare, they will not disband untill their demands are complied with." Still, we may guess Washington's growing concern when he learned in the course of the day that a second address was now winding its way through camp. At a minimum, it must have confirmed his own suspicions that its author was an agent not so much of the officers as of those who would use the officers as instruments to their own ends. A "double game," he wrote Jones, was being played, orchestrated in Philadelphia for the purposes of inciting "jealousies equally void of Foundation untill called into being by their vile Artificers." For the moment, he had stalled the crisis sure to come if more permanent solutions were not found. Washington thus pressed his friend in the city "to push this matter to an issue, and if there are Delegates among you, who are really opposed to doing justice to the Army, scruple not to tell them, if matters should come to extremity, that they must be answerable for all the ineffable horrors which may be occasioned thereby."[46]

In deferring the meeting to Saturday, Washington had hoped to buy some time and, more positively, to let emotions cool and to control for the unknown. Of course, the same strategy opened up more space for the anonymous author to press his plan. Two lines of reasoning order the second missive, each quite brilliant in its way. Professing himself aware of the delicate business at hand, the writer insisted that whatever the discomfort created by the first letter, it was the price to be paid in view of the stakes involved. If he had raised suspicions in the process, he would not apologize for that. Under the circumstances, suspicion was to be favored; though "detestable in private life," he argued, it is "the loveliest trait of political characters. It prompts to enquiry, bars the door against design, and opens every avenue to truth. It was the first to oppose a tyrant here, and still stands sentinel over the liberties of America—With this belief, it would illy become me, to stifle the voice of this honest guardian." Thus are rumor, resentment, and fear given the stamp of patriotism![47]

Though unlikely to assuage Washington's anxieties, such justifications may have had merit in the abstract. More galling, perhaps, was the ensuing attempt to seize upon the General's good intentions and turn them to advantage. Far from being put off by the General Orders of Tuesday, the author now explained, the officers ought to see in Washington's position a sign that he not only condoned the plan being forwarded but was in effect sanctioning it. After all, if the Commander in Chief had really wished to squelch the movement, he would not have called for the later meeting at all; by designating the procedures, leaders, and outcomes of the deliberations, he had added constituted authority to the entire affair. If anything, the new mode of operating would "give system to your proceedings, and stability to your resolves. It will ripen speculation onto fact, and while it adds to the unanimity, it cannot possibly lessen the independency, of your sentiments." Besides, the writer reasoned, the very fact that Washington wanted an official report of the meeting's resolves was evidence that they were thus "intended for Congress. Hence will arise another motive for that energy, which has been recommended." A clever gambit, but not clever enough: Washington would in short order seize and redirect "that energy" to his own ends and to the ultimate salvation of the army, the Revolution, and the country itself.[48]

Two day remained before the noon appointment at the Temple. On Thursday, March 13, Washington began in earnest to lay the groundwork for the work ahead. General Orders for the day dealt first with the court-martial of an unfortunate John Blasdell; for stealing shoes and boots from the clothing store he was to receive twenty-five lashes from each of three lines. That unpleasant business aside, Washington then enclosed a report from a congressional committee indicating that consideration had been given in late January to the officers' outstanding issues, including pay, settlement of several accounts, and commutation of half pay "for an equivalent in gross." The following resolutions announced that Superintendent Morris would be charged with conceiving a plan for delivery on pay and accounts. In the meantime, the men were to be assured that "Congress will make every effort in their power to obtain from the respective states substantial funds, adequate to the object of funding the whole debt of the United States, and will enter upon an immediate and full consideration of the nature of such funds, and the most likely mode of obtaining them." As for half pay and commutation, they would have to wait pending further efforts by a specially appointed committee. If the news did not palliate the officers, it may have at least signaled both their Commander's and Congress's good intentions. At the moment, Washington had little else to offer.[49]

Friday passed without incident. Although we have no record of his thoughts that day, we may surmise that he spent some of his time in reflection and anticipating what lay ahead. Following his example, we might similarly profit from taking a few steps back and getting a bit of perspective on the course of events thus far. First, it is clear from the record that nothing approaching outright treason was in the works. If we mean by that term an elaborate and premeditated design to achieve by stealth the subversion of rightful authority, then theorists of conspiracy are bound to be disappointed. The primary players in this game of pressure politics were of course bent on arrangements: that much is evident. The Morrises and Hamilton, chief among them, felt themselves and their country to be in dire circumstances, and they aimed to mobilize every resource they might muster to figure a way out of the bind. But they were just as unquestionably men of good faith, deeply committed to the cause of independence and the establishment of a viable republican government. The intelligence, energy, and personal capital expended on behalf of this cause is itself evidence of this commitment. Any talk of treason must be accordingly dismissed as nonsense.

At the same time, there can be no gainsaying that the nationalists hoped to push Washington against the wall. Thus fixed, he was to be forced to choose between the well-being of his officers and the dictates of military subordination. Those who sought to pressure the General, however, did not fully appreciate the fact that he was at his best under such circumstances. The previous chapter has sought to put on display those moments when, stressed on the one hand by the weight of his past and on the others by the demands of the future, Washington struggled to fashion a better version of himself and others. As a young man, he sought after the successes and failures of early military efforts to become less self-regarding and more mindful of others. Later, as an established planter and local grandee, he transformed himself from a largely private subject into a patriot on behalf of a cause greater than even himself. Still later, beset by the travails and despair of Valley Forge, Washington created the conditions of renewal and faith that were to lead the army out its hell and onto the fields of praise. And now the General found himself once more betwixt and between, confronted on one side by the claims of military fidelity and on the other by the most basic principles of civil government. Such circumstances operated not to constrain Washington but to most fully realize his unique capacities of character and persuasion.

An observation, finally, about these capacities. The following chapter offers a close reading of Washington's Newburgh Address of March 15, 1783. If the analysis has any merit, that speech will be seen to both reflect and instantiate the tenets thus far established. Here it may be useful by way of transition only to suggest a general strategy for understanding the rhetorical work of the address. Military historians have frequently characterized Washington's field operations as "Fabian," that is, as exemplifying the tactical wizardry of the third-century B.C.E. Roman general Fabius Maximus. Fabius's singular talent was to make of weakness a strength by capitalizing on rapid maneuver and ingenious timing and by outwitting larger and more powerful enemies. Those who would push this line of thinking see in Washington a similar faculty at work: confronted by the mightiest military force on earth, he mastered in time the art of retreat, the lightening assault, and the end-around in such a way as to secure ultimate victory. When this approach works, it does so because it changes the rules of the game;

it refuses to abide by what is putatively a given and demands to be engaged on altogether different terms. The effect is to beggar the enemy's store of resources and conventional wisdom and to create new possibilities for success.

Washington's Newburgh Address might well be understood as the rhetorical equivalent of Fabius's martial art. Without wishing to push the analogy too far, we can yet see in his speech a characteristic refusal to accept the logic of large-scale confrontation. Rather, he maneuvers to advantage; strikes quickly to define and then contain the enemy; deprives him of his usual sources of strength; limits losses on both sides; and emerges strong enough to carry the battle another day.

CHAPTER 3

"By the dignity of your conduct"

The Newburgh Address and the Language of Character

The settlement no longer remains, but the memory endures. In 206 B.C.E. the Roman army encamped itself near Sucro, in southeastern Spain. The Second Punic War, despite initial reverses, was fast coming to an end with recent Roman victories and the final defeat of the Carthaginians earlier in the year. Eight thousand troops under the generalship of P. Cornelius Scipio lay garrisoned, with time on their hands and resentments to nurture. Such satisfaction as the triumph may have afforded soured over lack of pay, length of service, and paucity of supplies. Soon enough rumors circulated through camp that Scipio was dying or dead, that Spanish allies were in open revolt, and that now was the perfect time to stage a mutiny on behalf of their grievances. Livy reports that some thirty-five conspirators among them set the plan in motion, certain "that P. Scipio, after the favour the gods had shown him, and, indeed, the whole State, would show their gratitude." They did not. Learning of the design upon his authority, Scipio summoned the army and excoriated its weakness, accused it of mass insanity, and decried its lack of honor. He then had the ringleaders brought forward; they were "tied to the stake, scourged, and finally beheaded. The spectators were so benumbed by terror," Livy noted, "that no voice was raised against the severity of the punishment, not even a groan was heard."[1]

That is one way to deal with unrest in the ranks. And, truth be told, it bears the sanction of the ages. Mutiny breeds anarchy, from which, Antigone knew, cities tumble, great houses rain down, and armies scatter. But it is not the only way, and history teaches us as well that such evils are not really fated, that the moment of crisis can mean not the end of moral order but can provide the very conditions of its rebirth. Readers of Livy will recall that in the end Scipio, in his way, forgave the army and worked to ameliorate its hardship. But the point is those ringleaders had to die, and they had to die in spectacular fashion. There is justice of a kind here, and mercy as well. We might even say that it all worked out, at least in the short run. Washington's address before the officers at Newburgh offers us an opportunity to see a rather different way in which discontent within the army can be handled. It too features considerations of justice and mercy, and it too worked out in the short run. Two more different speeches would be hard to imagine, however. We need not extend the parallel beyond its due date, but we can at least observe the lasting image of one general gazing over his men and seeing there a threat to be ended and the other, gazing, a force powerful enough to change the world.[2]

———— • ————

Newburgh, New York, sits on the Hudson River some ten miles north of West Point. Nestled there among the Highlands, it commands a long and bracing view of the river—an excellent position, then, for keeping an eye on any threat from north or south. Here virtually the entire Army of the United States arrived to wait out peace negotiations in Paris, and here Washington settled into the old Hasbrouck house, where he was to remain from April 1782 until he took leave in August 1783. By late October 1782 the army—sixteen regiments numbering more than ten thousand men in all, was fully encamped in huts that measured fourteen by sixteen by six feet, spread out over several miles along the river's edge. In time most of the leading officers would join Washington there, including Wayne, Putman, Sullivan, Greene, Knox, Heath, Lafayette, Steuben, and Hamilton, along with Mrs. Washington and such luminaries as the Marquis de Lafayette and the Marquis de Chastellux. Featured prominently in its midst was "The Temple," constructed by order of General Heath and serving as a central meeting place for devotion, amusement, and deliberation. Eighty feet long, forty feet wide, and fifteen feet high, the building was large enough to accommodate upwards of seven hundred men. Freemasons in the region were known to gather there; later, the Order of the Cincinnati was first conceived under its roof. We know it, of course, as the site wherein Washington stepped forward to deliver the most consequential speech of his career.[3]

In the course of his stay, the longest of his military career, the General was to compose at Newburgh some of his most memorable productions, including, early, his response to the importunings of Colonel Nicola and, later, his Circular to the States. In the meantime, he sat and waited, and he grew increasingly concerned over the state of his army and, especially, its officer corps. "The evils of which they complain," he wrote to the Secretary at War, "and which they suppose almost remidiless, are the total want of money, or the means of existing from one day to the other, the heavy debts they have already incurred, the loss of credit, the distress of their families at home, and the prospect of poverty and misery before them. You may rely upon it," Washington warned, "the patriotism and long suffering of this army are almost exhausted, and there never was so great a spirit of discontent as at this instant." Washington, to be sure, had been posting such dire warnings for the entirety of the war, and we may forgive his many supporters in Congress if they found a certain predictability in the letters. Washington was nevertheless dead serious about the perilous condition of his army. He knew full well that no amount of parading and pep talks could resolve the very real grievances it harbored. Every indication from the available record reveals a persistent anxiety that matters were fast reaching a state of crisis and that if Congress did not act, his officers would. In charting the arc of events leading to March 1783, we have seen that indeed Congress—or a small part of it—was in fact very much in action, seeking and finding through the army's discontent a lever with which to move the states and other recalcitrant forces toward resolution of a kind.[4]

The challenge thus posed to Washington could not have been greater. He had faced mutiny among the ranks before and dealt with them swiftly and effectively. This much was fully within his power, buttressed by military precedent, law, and force of arms. The crisis of March 1783 was altogether different. In confronting it, the General had recourse to nothing except his own resources, his own authority, and the moral weight that authority could be seen to wield. What he must do he must say: that is, the problem was rhetorical through and through. This fact presents us with several challenges of our own, not least in coming to terms with Washington as not only a doer of deeds but a speaker of words. Although it threatens to defer direct engagement with the Newburgh Address, this challenge must be dealt with before we can proceed further. It will help at this point to keep in mind what we are about: to see in Washington's speech this day the fullest expression of his rhetorical craft, in which he so fashions an image of moral order as to induce his audience to act on its own best sense of itself on behalf of something greater than itself.

Our task is met first by locating Washington's effort within the rhetorical landscape of late-eighteenth-century America. The survey must be quite general, but it will be sufficient to help contextualize not only the role of the speaker but his audience and speech as well. To begin, we need to clear some ground. The period was of course alive with words; few epochs before our noisy age could rival the revolutionary era in the sheer amount, quality, and power of language it produced. It was not, to be sure, a time notable for literary achievements conventionally understood, as contemporaries well knew and often fretted over. They need not and did not, however, have anything to apologize for when it came to the arts of public address. Certain broad tendencies may be identified to account for this rhetorical efflorescence. Among the white population, colonists enjoyed relative prosperity, positive social mobility, and increasingly widespread levels of at least rudimentary education. These markers of cultural growth in turn help explain exceptionally high rates of literacy and, not coincidentally, a rich and flourishing print media. Although the colonies/states would remain overwhelming rural, an advanced postal system kept open lines of communication from Georgia to New Hampshire. For their part, towns and cities featured a variety of locales for the airing of citizens' voices, from the tea shop to the ale house, from the printer's office to the street corner, from kingdom hall to town hall.[5]

It would be difficult to imagine a more fertile ground for debating matters of empire. As Bernard Bailyn and others have amply demonstrated, the decade before the outbreak of armed hostilities produced an extraordinary outpouring of broadsides, newspaper pieces, pamphlets, books, songs, poetry, and visual texts; so too with sermons, speeches from the bar, and political orations. For good reason, we have looked back on this time as something of a golden age of American rhetoric. There is James Otis, declaiming against the writs of assistance; there Sam Adams penning the words—it must be said—of treason; Patrick Henry thundering before astonished crowds; there Thomas Paine brazenly thumbing his nose at His Majesty. And, of course, there is Thomas Jefferson, yielding to the world language not even he could control. Even the doggerel verse and the amateurish political theory, the rustic's letter to the editor and the crude lampoons: these too evince a kind of color and confidence in the arts of persuasion that must be appreciated.

Just where Washington fits—if at all—into this bracing and boisterous scene is not readily apparent. Clearly, as we have already noted, he was no orator, at least in the sense suggested by the likes of Henry and Otis. Nor was he a polemicist or a pamphleteer along the lines of an Adams or a Paine; nor was he capable of the conceptual felicity we associate with a Jefferson or a Madison. All this is quite true and might seem to limit severely claims as to Washington's rhetorical legacy. But it is true only in a very restricted sense, and here I wish to be as clear as possible. First, I am not interested in advancing any thesis about the Eloquence of George Washington, not being convinced that much if anything is gained in doing so. Second and more important, situating the Newburgh Address in such a context imposes an alien and inappropriate standard of judgment. As a product of the Virginia landed elite, Washington would naturally have been averse to the populist implications of many rhetorical forms. Gentlemen—and Sam Adams, Thomas Paine, and even Patrick Henry were no gentleman—did not carry on so. Third, the Newburgh Address was delivered under conditions that in no sense are to be confused with the civil and political ambitions of the patriot cause. It was very much concerned with civil principles, of course, and carried with profound implications for republican polity. But it was perforce a military address delivered to an officer corps gathered at the end of a war of liberation.[6]

Washington's address is thus best read not so much as an example of early American oratory in general but as a distinctive rhetorical performance rendered within unprecedented circumstances. This much takes us a small step at least toward a more positive construction of the speech, its meaning, and how we are to understand it. The key term here is performance, by which I mean to stress the ways in which the speaker embodies and articulates the very principles he would have his audience assume. To underscore the point, we can ask the assistance of Sandra Gustafson, who has thought long and written well on these matters. Gustafson prefers to frame the sense of rhetoric I am after as a form of *enactment,* which she parses out as "performativity, or the power of words themselves to effect a result, an idealized moment when language and action unite fully in an agent; and performance, or the pervasive theatricality that opens a space between intention and realization, calling into question the possibility of their full union." This image of the speaker embodying the speech and thus creating the conditions of its own resolution is key to grasping the rhetorical force of Washington's address. My treatment seeks to strengthen that grasp by being mindful of the tensions that sustain its structure and meaning. These tensions have been identified as emerging from the spaces between endings and beginnings, and they focus our attention on questions of honor, conviction, and the drama of rebirth. The ends of speech thus conceptualized require that the speaker and the audience become, in a sense, one. We need accordingly to establish a perspective on the status and function of Washington's audience. That accomplished, we will move then to a close reading of the text itself.[7]

From the moment of his appointment as commander in chief, Washington was clear about his expectations. His officers were to be men of character and reputation, of demonstrable merit and evident promise. And while it is true that they were notably short on martial experience, that they were chosen for political as well as strictly military reasons, and that they could prove an exasperating lot, the officers in the end earned their leader's enduring regard. Washington got on well with most of them, though not all. His inner circle was intensely devoted to him, indeed so much so that some critics feared the unwonted influence of Henry Knox, Lafayette, Nathanael Greene, and others. Gates he must endure; Charles Lee he could not. In the early years of the war, the General might despair over the amateur tendencies and excesses of these men; by now, most of the chaff had been winnowed, and he could with reason look upon his audience as a battle-hardened, loyal assembly of fellow officers.

With few exceptions, the Newburgh officers were as Washington hoped: soldiers, yes, but citizens above all.

Like Sam Adams, they were well aware that "history affords abundant instances of established armies making themselves the masters of those countries which they were designed to protect." They were proving exceptions to the rule. They came forward not from a European-style military caste but from the cities, villages, and farms of colonial America. Believing their cause just, they sacrificed material gain and physical comfort for a set of ideas, abstractions, perhaps, but principles they knew would help create a better world for themselves, their families, and their neighbors. Along the way these men showed themselves to be fast learners, possessed of a certain agility of mind and improvisational intelligence. When they faltered, which they surely did, they rose again and pressed on. At moments they were capable of astonishing feats of valor and endurance: Knox retrieving the artillery at Ticonderoga; Greene in South Carolina; Morgan at Cowpens. Just as important, they *endured.* They endured the ignominy of Long Island and New York, the Pennsylvania campaign and Valley Forge, the winters of Morristown and the southern defeats. Those who could not keep the faith were gone; those who remained were proud of their achievement, and rightfully so.[8]

But wars effect changes in men no less than ideologies, none more so than revolutionary wars. Whatever embers remained of the *rage militaire* that once burned so brightly were by now dying fast or dead. The years of privation, penury, and suspicion; the unending struggle to sustain a viable and long-term army; the battles with Congress over supply, rank, pay, and pensions: it was all too much. We will have missed the full import of these resentments, however explicable, if we limit them to matters of material provision and financial compensation. The officers of Newburgh were restive—and vulnerable—because their pride had been in some sense deeply wounded. Alexander McDougall thus spoke for his class when he declared that "The American Generals . . . are subject to the most illiterate Athenian Caprice and abuse and . . . their reputations Calumniated by many who have not taken the Field." The Newburgh crisis was wrought by a culmination of this kind of resentment, as much against the honor thought due to the officers as against sheer physical hardship. No officer, for that matter, had ever gone hungry or naked. The wound was to a conception of who they were and what they were owed. The pensions and pay issue were but tokens of a greater crisis of identity itself. "By the end of the war," Richard Kohn concludes, "the resentment, the feeling of maltreatment and victimization—the sense of martyrdom—was widespread. The wonder of the officers' near revolt at Newburgh in 1783 was not that it happened, but that it was so long in the coming."[9]

The revolutionary officer corps, like military classes since time out of mind, sustained itself on a steady diet of resentments against its civilian counterpart. "The Rascally Stupidity which now prevails in the Country at large," announced one such plaintiff, "is beyond all description." Many others voiced similar if less strident complaints. Predictably, civilians themselves nurtured their own resentments against a body they deemed just as "Rascally." In addition to fears of military overreach and presumption, ordinary Americans lamented depredations upon their land and goods, restriction of their rights, and impositions upon family and community. For many, both military and civilian, the question of who now could claim the mantle of revolutionary virtue seemed at stake. The officers, isolated and unappreciated, bolstered by a heightened esprit de corps, perceived themselves to be the last bastion of the values for which the war was being fought. Put-upon civilians in turn saw themselves as the genuine repository of American virtue. When they witnessed a military elite now demanding more than they were willing to give, they necessarily interpreted the pension issue as a confirmation of their deepest anxieties about armies in general.[10]

Here then was an audience to behold in any number of ways. We cannot provide a complete or detailed profile of the group before Washington, as large and diverse as it must have been. It may be suggestive, nevertheless, to attempt some indication of the range of perspectives present in the room. Having pointed to several traits we can plausibly say the officers possessed in common, what can we say about their differences? One way of answering the question, admittedly limited, is to take a brief look at three men, distinctive enough, to be sure, but representative of certain possibilities inherent to Washington's task. To this end, let us fix our eyes on one officer whose relationship to the speaker had been less than comfortable through the years, one who had enjoyed Washington's closest confidence and respect, and finally a figure neither at odds with nor close to the General.

No revolutionary general save Benedict Arnold has suffered more at the hands of historians than Horatio Gates (1727–1806). A "little ruddy-faced Englishman," "unctuously pious," possessed of a "repellant personality," "an old, granny-looking fellow," an "ugly nearsighted, stocky, aggressive captain," Gates seems physically to have embodied the defects so readily attached to his name. At first glance this hardly seems fair: together with Charles Lee, he could boast of far greater military service than any other general, and his range of service, including action in Europe, Canada, the Caribbean, and the Northern, Eastern, and Southern Departments during the war, was without rival. Gates proved an excellent administrator, enjoyed considerable popularity among the soldiers, and of course was widely—and wildly—heralded as the victor of Saratoga.[11]

Born in Kent County, England, he advanced quickly through the ranks and made his mark early. Stymied by British protocols of appointment, he made his way to the colonies in 1769 and was named brigadier general and Washington's adjutant in the summer of 1775. Inevitably, perhaps, Gates's intense desire to be near the action meant that he would lose as well as gain by proximity to power. For all his assets, he seemed chronically unable to get along with other forceful personalities and battled to no good effect fellow officers ranging from Philip Schuyler to Arnold. Although the "Conway Cabal" has largely been discredited as a serious challenge to Washington's authority, Gates could not escape being implicated in the alleged plot to replace to the General. The air around that so-called conspiracy was cleared soon enough, but Gates's reputation never really recovered. With the chance to redeem himself at Camden in the summer of 1780, Gates suffered a terrible loss at the hands of Cornwallis and from there beat a hasty and notorious retreat from the carnage. Congress, the object of so much of Gates's hectoring through the years, initiated an inquiry into his command at Camden; nothing came of it, but, again, the damage had been done. The lingering days of the war found him in Newburgh, close by the General to whom he had once so abjectly apologized. What could possibly have been passing through his mind this midday of March 15 we will never know, nor shall we know of his pre-cise role in bringing events to this critic juncture. He was by this point a sad and beaten man, frustrated by the fates and his own limitations. In time Gates would retire to the pleasures of New York and its social and political bustle. For now, all he could do was listen, closely.[12]

The scene is indelible and tells us much about the relationship between His Excellency and his chief artillery officer. Struggling, unsuccessfully, to control his emotions, Washington rises before his men in the tavern and asks that each come forward. The officer closest approaches first and offers his hand, and the two then tearfully embrace. It is perfect in every way, capturing as it does the pathos of years and love of a kind. If we need look for Gates's opposite, then surely it is to be found in the ample figure of Henry Knox (1750–1806), Wash-ington's righthand man for the entirety of the war and indeed beyond. He was there with his commander during the siege of Boston, with him in New York, at Trenton and Princeton, through the battles of Brandywine and Germantown, at Monmouth, and finally at Yorktown. Through it all Knox seems never to have incurred Washington's censure. Professionally, there can be little wonder in this: Knox had proved not only indefatigable in the service of the cause but invaluable as its leading artillery engineer and strategist. Personally, the two men, so differ-ent in so many respects, formed one of the great military friendships in American history.[13]

Henry Knox, who was to play his own key role in the Newburgh crisis, had come to this moment through a remarkable route. Of modest family origins, he managed through native talent and grit to establish himself in Boston as the owner of the London Book Store, where, the story has it, he immersed himself deeply in military lore. The city was soon enough to offer plenty of the real thing for his bookish imagination to play on, and he quickly insinuated himself into its militia culture and organized resistance. After Bunker Hill, where he directed artillery operations, Knox befriended Washington and secured his lasting regard through his implausible trek for the guns of Ticonderoga. From there it is a story of unceasing activity alongside the Commander in Chief; when not in or preparing for actual battle, Knox found the time and energy to organize training programs, armory dispositions, and other military logistics. There were a few bumps, to be sure: the row over du Coudray's appointment as head of artillery and the unfortunate decisions at Germantown. But otherwise Knox's record of accomplishment was unassailable, and for this the portly bookseller from Boston was promoted to major general early in 1782. After Newburgh, Knox succeeded Benjamin Lincoln as Secretary of War and continued to serve in that office during the nation's tumultuous early years. All this suggests, reasonably, that in Knox Washington had the most supportive listener in the room. Even so, he too had a part to play, and he needed to play it convincingly and well.[14]

If Gates and Knox may be positioned at far ends of an affinitive spectrum, William Heath (1737–1814) falls somewhere toward the middle. He is thus useful as a point of perspective from which we can glimpse perhaps the large midsection of Washington's immediate audience. Heath was neither, as far as we know, disaffected with his general nor especially close to him, although he had been on the scene since the outset of armed hostilities. Born to an old family in Roxbury, Massachusetts, Heath early in his adult life complemented his farming labors with minor political offices and served as a captain of the Suffolk County militia. Fat, bald, and unassuming, the middle-aged planter nevertheless asserted himself to some effect early in the war by assisting in the siege of Boston and thereafter helped lead the army to its unfortunate appointment in New York.[15]

While promoted in due course to major general in the summer of 1776, Heath seems not to have impressed Washington overmuch and was displaced from the center of action. He did manage to lead—if that is the word for it—the engagement at Fort Independence in January 1777. It did not go well. Timothy Pickering reported of Heath that he "has, in the estimate of every discerning man, acquired nothing but disgrace." More mortifying, surely, Washington himself informed Heath that "your conduct is censured . . . as being fought with too much caution by which the Army has been disappointed, and in some degree disgraced." Overmatched and lacking obvious military talents, Heath still retained a reputation as an "honest, obstinate man," in General Spencer's view, and would be not only retained but put to quiet service east of the Hudson, where he exercised his modest talents by directing the construction of the Temple. After the signing of the peace treaty, Heath returned home to a life of moderate prosperity and a series of minor political offices.[16]

Like many in Washington's audience, then, General Heath thus found himself with no real axe to grind with the speaker himself. True, his record had not been stellar, and he had been roundly scolded by his Commander in Chief, and that is never pleasant. But his wartime experience had not been altogether negative: he had proved himself a patriot, had materially assisted in the war's prosecution, had managed to stay alive and to endure to the end. He had given eight years to his new country, and though he had not covered himself in glory, he had played his role in the unfolding drama of the age. General Heath, it may be said, had earned every bit of his claim on the nation's conscious. He was no hero, but he was a man of honor, an officer to whom honor was due. Washington must have known this, and he had to speak to this reality. Three men only, vastly different in temperament, achievement, and affinity to the General: they yet hint at something of the complexity of Washington's rhetorical task, designed as it must be to find a common denominator among their obvious differences.

——— • ———

Time now to turn our attention to the address proper. Here I will provide a brief description of its general characteristics and proceed to a more detailed analysis. It is a short speech—1,632 words total—and, though phrased in conventional eighteenth-century prose, is, as we would expect of Washington, direct and lacking any ostentation. At its most general, the text may be seen as operating through a simple but devastating logic of difference and identity, wherein a series of initial juxtapositions opens the way for a final restoration of a moral order that has come under threat. The rhetorical action of the text may thus be seen as collaboration between form and content, through which a play of disjunctions ultimately gives meaning and force to the message as a whole. We are obliged, then, to attend to each of its nine paragraphs closely and in seriatim; this manner of proceeding will require a certain patience, but it will be rewarded if we can thus capture the dynamics of the performance. We are not looking at a poem here, and any claim to subtly must be balanced by attention to the speaker's public and practical ends. Still, we are in a position now to observe the workings of argument conspicuous for its craft and artistic design. My aim is not to gloss or paraphrase the text—it will be represented in its entirety—but to identity the work it may be seen to effect.[17]

Our key to understanding the rhetorical economy of the speech rests in locating the space created by the rendering of incommensurable alternatives. It is precisely in this space, again, that Washington can be seen inserting himself as the ultimate means to the resolution of a dilemma that would remain otherwise intolerable. In the end, Washington was accordingly able to confront the enemy, to expose him and anticipate the rebarbative consequences of the conspiracy, and to assure his audience that it held the key to managing the crisis to optimal effect. That he was able not only to create this possibility, to not only open this space, but to fill it and thus defuse the Newburgh crisis cannot be accounted for in terms other than sheer force of character as such. As evidence for this claim, I offer the following analysis.

ANALYSIS OF THE TEXT
Paragraph

[1] By an anonymous summons, an attempt has been made to convene you together; how inconsistent with the rules of propriety! how unmilitary! and how subversive of all order and discipline, let the good sense of the Army decide.

Here is classic Washington prose: the language simple and direct, the sentiment clear, and the gesture unmistakable. From the very outset, the speaker alerts his audience not only that he has been made aware of the situation but that he fully comprehends its meaning and portent. The fact that the crisis is fed by an *anonymous* source will be key as the address unfolds; for now it is announced so early as to color all that is to follow. At this point, it may seem odd that Washington decries such anonymity first as an affront to military protocol. Students of Washington will appreciate, however, that matters of propriety were for the General exceedingly important; why they were so important is foreshadowed in his appeal to *order.* We note, finally, the effort made to cast the officers themselves as players in this drama: possessed as they are of "good sense," the men can be trusted to understand the situation and to act accordingly. Thus, though brief, the introductory passage has already alerted us to a set of key considerations: (1) the symbolic implications of anonymity; (2) the importance of proper procedure; and (3) the legitimacy of the moral order and the agency of the officers at hand. We will keep these in mind as the speech progresses.

[2] In the moment of this Summons, another anonymous production was sent into circulation, addressed more to the feelings and passions, than to the reason and judgment of the Army. The author of the piece, is entitled to much credit for the goodness of his Pen and I could wish he had as much credit for the rectitude of his Heart, for, as Men see thro' different Optics, and are induced by the reflecting faculties of the Mind, to use different means, to attain the same end, the Author of the Address,

should have had more charity, than to mark for Suspicion, the Man who should recommend moderation and longer forbearance, or, in other words, who should not think as he thinks, and act as he advises. But he had another plan in view, in which candor and liberality of Sentiment, regard to justice, and love of Country, have no part; and he was right, to insinuate the darkest suspicion, to effect the blackest designs.

The opening phase sets itself immediately to the task of identifying the source of the conspiracy, unknown by person though he may be. Now Washington, crucially, sets to coaching the officers in how it is to be made sense of. An insidious and unknown force has invaded the camp: though effected by design, it betokens chaos; though artful, it claims no author; though seductive, it promises not satisfaction but ruin. We thus note at the outset a telling strategy: no blame is placed on the officers themselves, no fault, no stigma. I will comment on this fact later, but here we see that it provides clean access to the target at hand. After stressing the anonymous and unauthorized nature of the letters that had been winding their way through camp, Washington reinforces the sense that he is in command—that he is onto the game.

What are we to make of the reference to the anonymous writer's arts of address? Looking back on the event months later, Washington would again stress the craft with which the letters were composed. The letters, he then believed, had, "in point of composition, in elegance and force of expression," "rarely been equalled in the English Language." At first glance it hardly seems to bear mentioning that the insurgent was equipped with a capable pen. On reflection, however, we see that the allusion is wholly consistent with a more general emphasis on the juxtaposition of the hidden and the apparent, where such art is but a mask for subterfuge, a confusion of craft with craftiness. This too is part of the coaching Washington undertakes, as if to instruct his audience in how to read conspiracy. The ocular imagery here is suggestive, serving as it does to remind the audience that it is equipped not just to see but to see through. The author's identity is thus fixed, though nameless, as his designs come into view; his techniques of insinuation have been betrayed by his own ends.

[3] That the Address is drawn with great Art, and is designed to answer the most insidious purposes. That it is calculated to impress the Mind, with an idea of premeditated injustice in the Sovereign power of the United States, and rouse all those resentments which must unavoidably flow from such a belief. That the secret mover of this Scheme (whoever he may be) intended to take advantage of the passions, while they were warmed by the recollection of past distresses, without giving time

for cool, deliberative thinking, and that composure of Mind which is
so necessary to give dignity and stability to measures is rendered too
obvious, by the mode of conducting the business, to need other proof
than a reference to the preceeding.

The speaker has by now moved his audience into a position to see, thus to discern
behind the mask of artful design the insidious purposes at work. Once exposed,
the agent in their midst presents himself with unwitting clarity; indeed, no
further proof is required, and Washington claims the luxury of his assumption.
In very quick order he sets into play a series of differentiations that will help
structure the address as a whole. Far from indicting the officers for any complicity in the plot, he rather works to drive a wedge between them and the unseen
and unnamed forces in their midst. Where the officers are present, the enemy is
unknown; reason vies against passion, responsibility wars with dishonor, stead-
fastness with intrigue. The looming sense of plot, scheme, and conspiracy are
scarcely incidental to the work of the address, and if these suspicions bear a certain resemblance to the rhetoric of resistance on the eve of revolution, that too is
wholly explicable. Washington and virtually all patriots were deeply versed in the
language of conspiracy and the distinctive logics by which it operates. Hence the
recurrent references to "art," "design," "darkest suspicion," to plans and "blackest
designs," "insideous purposes," calculation, secrecy, premeditation, schemes, and
plots. Over and against this concerted and covert design to unsettle the resolve
of the officers, Washington contrasts their "candor and liberality of sentiments,"
their proven "regard for justice and love of country," the "cool, deliberative thinking and composure of mind," their "dignity and stability."

Washington need not detail at length further evidence of the plot: speaker
and audience are at one in grasping all that is necessary to fix the source and the
plan. We note again the aggregation of opposites, in which appearance is set off
against reality, secrecy against disclosure, passion against reasoned composure.
These juxtapositions again will accumulate to decisive effect throughout the address: formally and morally, they will in this way create a clearing among the
press of events and anxieties, a space into which the speaker will ultimately assert
himself. But there is further work to be done.

[4] Thus much, Gentlemen, I have thought it incumbent on me to observe
to you, to shew upon what principles I opposed the irregular and hasty
meeting which was proposed to have been held on Tuesday last: and not
because I wanted a disposition to give you every opportunity consistent
with your own honor, and the dignity of the Army, to make known your
grievances. If my conduct heretofore, has not evinced to you, that I have

been a faithful friend to the Army, my declaration of it at this time wd. be equally unavailing and improper. But as I was among the first who embarked in the cause of our common Country. As I have never left your side one moment, but when called from you on public duty. As I have been the constant companion and witness of your Distresses, and not among the last to feel, and acknowledge your Merits. As I have ever considered my own Military reputation as inseperably connected with that of the Army. As my Heart has ever expanded with joy, when I have heard its praises, and my indignation has arisen, when the mouth of detraction has been opened against it, it can *scarcely be supposed,* at this late stage of the War, that I am indifferent to its interests. But, how are they to be promoted? The way is plain, says the anonymous Addresser. If War continues, remove into the unsettled Country; there establish yourselves, and leave an ungrateful Country to defend itself. But who are they to defend? Our Wives, our Children, our Farms, and other property which we leave behind us. Or, in this state of hostile seperation, are we to take the two first (the latter cannot be removed), to perish in a Wilderness, with hunger, cold and nakedness? If Peace takes place, never sheath your Swords Says he untill you have obtained full and ample justice; this dreadful alternative, of either deserting our Country in the extremest hour of her distress, or turning our Arms against it, (which is the apparent object, unless Congress can be compelled into instant compliance) has something so shocking in it, that humanity revolts at the idea. My God! what can this writer have in view, by recommending such measures? Can he be a friend to the Army? Can he be a friend to this Country? Rather, is he not an insidious Foe? Some Emissary, perhaps, from New York, plotting the ruin of both, by sowing the seeds of discord and seperation between the Civil and Military powers of the Continent? And what a Compliment does he pay to our Understandings, when he recommends measures in either alternative, impracticable in their Nature?

Here is the longest and perhaps most complex paragraph of the address. It will require careful parsing, but if we are patient, we will detect in it the key to Washington's performance generally. Its first half is devoted exclusively to his own role in the events leading to the crisis at hand. By way of contrast, it is worth noting that this is the first such self-reference of the speech; in fact, Washington registers thirteen first-person pronouns in only three (long) sentences. The General was not in the habit of defending himself: he was not often called upon to do so, and he seems to have felt no particular need to justify his actions during the years of battle. If anything, Washington could be rather thin-skinned about criticism, real or perceived. We cannot read these lines, therefore, as in any sense constituting an apologia or even an effort toward redemption. What then is he up to here?

The second letter winding its way through camp, it will be recalled, insinuated without using his name that Washington had shown himself less than enthusiastic about the proposed gathering of officers. Prudent to a fault, Washington, it seemed, was bent on dithering away such opportunities as might give real voice to the officers' perfectly legitimate complaints: hence the squelching of the Wednesday meeting. Nonsense, insists Washington. He will neither seek to excuse himself nor explain away his actions. The very fact that the men are assembled now is proof that he is willing to entertain their grievances. More important, the challenge to his authority invites the speaker to underscore his essential identity with his officers, their hardships, hopes, and deepest commitments. Washington, of course, knows that the incipient mutiny is not against his person; still, he seizes this occasion to stress that he has after all signed on at the very beginning; has never taken leave of the army; has suffered alongside his officers every step of the way; has acknowledged their valor; has considered their triumphs and defeats as his own. The significance of this passage to the overall economy of the address cannot be missed: embedded in this short declaration of affinities is a set of values that he will shortly invite his audience to assume with him: faith, gratitude, friendship, perseverance, fellow-feeling, sacrifice, honor.

Against this array of positives now contend the negative claims of the insurgent. Whoever he may be, he has by now been contained—the source of much danger, to be sure, but not evidently representative of any more general discontent. Still, a force to be confronted, and Washington now moves to give practical consideration to his designs. His case in effect takes the form of a reductio ad absurdum, expressed through a disjunctive syllogism. The mysterious author offers up two alternatives: if war persists, then the officers are to take their men into the wilderness; if peace arrives, then they are to keep their arms in defiance of civil order. The disjunction is self-evidently false and pernicious. The former option necessarily means abandoning not only the country but kith and kin to the ravages of the enemy; the latter is little short of treason. Washington professes himself incredulous at the sheer idiocy of the plan, a shock to common humanity and working only to sow "seeds of discord and seperation [sic] between the Civil and Military powers of the continent." On the one side, then, such principles as embodied in the person of Washington; on the other, such portents of danger as revealed in the insurgent.

[5] But here, Gentlemen, I will drop the curtain, because it wd. be as imprudent in me to assign my reasons for this opinion, as it would be

insulting to your conception, to suppose you stood in need of them. A moment's reflection will convince every dispassionate Mind of the physical impossibility of carrying either proposal into execution.

Washington will not, of course, "drop the curtain," at least not on the occasion before him. But he will have done with source of the threat, the machinations and intrigue. The paragraph, though brief, signals a pivot in the direction of the address: the provocation has been identified, rendered intelligible, contained, contrasted, and renounced for its implications. Here the speech shifts to a broader set of considerations regarding the responsibilities incumbent upon speaker and audience; at question now is the optimal relationship between them and what that relationship may provide by way of final resolution.

> [6] There might, Gentlemen, be an impropriety in my taking notice, in this Address to you, of an anonymous production, but the manner in which that performance has been introduced to the Army, the effect it was intended to have, together with some other circumstances, will amply justify my observations on the tendency of that Writing. With respect to the advice given by the Author, to suspect the Man, who shall recommend moderate measures and longer forbearance, I spurn it, as every Man, who regards that liberty, and reveres that justice for which we contend, undoubtedly must; for if Men are to be precluded from offering their Sentiments on a matter, which may involve the most serious and alarming consequences, that can invite the consideration of Mankind, reason is of no use to us; the freedom of Speech may be taken away, and, dumb and silent we may be led, like sheep, to the Slaughter.

Though he will not apologize, he will explain. This much Washington feels himself obligated to do. He and the officers know that discontent is an inevitable fact of military life, know too that the Commander in Chief cannot reasonably be expected to concern himself with every challenge to his authority or to the dignity of the army. But some threats are greater than others, and the General cannot wave away this one. Needless to say, all this has put the General in a precarious position: if he shows himself a supporter of the disaffected, he courts suspicion as to his own motives; if he resists their efforts too forcefully, he may well alienate their affections. Under these pressures, moderation itself will not satisfy, and of this Hamilton had warned a month earlier in a letter to Washington: "An idea is propagated in the army," he wrote in mid-February 1783, "that delicacy carried to an extreme prevents your espousing its interests with sufficient warmth. The falsehood of this opinion no one can be better acquainted with than yourself; but it is not the less mischievous for being false."

To the extent that the Newburgh plot, in part, cast the speaker in a less than favorable light, it might bear attention; to the extent that in doing so it could give the officers reason to doubt, it *must* be addressed. In doing so and because of the manner in which it is executed, Washington sets up the final phases of the speech, in which he takes up, respectively, himself, Congress, and ultimately his audience. As for the image of Washington before the men, much of that work has already been completed; the speaker now need only clarify his own motives and secure his ends with theirs.

> [7] I cannot, in justice to my own belief, and what I have great reason to conceive is the intention of Congress, conclude this Address, without giving it as my decided opinion, that that Honorable Body, entertain exalted sentiments of the Services of the Army; and, from a full conviction of its merits and sufferings, will do it compleat justice. That their endeavors, to discover and establish funds for this purpose, have been unwearied, and will not cease, till they have succeeded, I have not a doubt. But, like all other large Bodies, where there is a variety of different Interests to reconcile, their deliberations are slow. Why then should we distrust them? and, in consequence of that distrust, adopt measures, which may cast a shade over that glory which, has been so justly acquired; and tarnish the reputation of an Army which is celebrated thro' all Europe, for its fortitude and Patriotism? and for what is this done? to bring the object we seek nearer? No! most certainly, in my opinion, it will cast it at a greater distance.

Here the transition to Congress's role is key to the unfolding dynamics of the address. In appreciating its function, we need to bear in mind the speaker's general ambition: to give his audience a reason to believe. That task, as we have seen, is made the more vexing because in truth that audience has been asked to believe for so long and with such little demonstrable return on the investment that further such pleas may well seem hollow at best, cynical at worst. The challenge is made greater, as result, because Washington must seek the officers' trust as a matter of faith. Lacking a credible track record of congressional support, they are being ask to step down on the *promise* of justice not yet rendered. The only conceivable basis for such a faith, for believing in that promise, rests in the moral authority of the speaker before them. They have nothing else. Their trust is hence to be leveraged on the fulcrum of Washington's own character.

Historians have not been especially kind to the wartime Congress, and its sundry shortcoming have been already treated. More sympathetic commentators have stressed the very real constraints under which it had to operate, its lack of traditional authority, and its good-faith efforts on behalf of the army in general. Even granting this more positive interpretation, there can be no gainsaying the intense resentment, bordering on contempt, directed by the officers at Congress for its role in the army's hardships. In asking his men to believe, in short, Washington was asking a great deal indeed. Sensing this, perhaps, Washington at this moment retrieved a letter from his pocket, a missive from Philadelphia assuring the men of Congress's good-faith intentions to do right by their demands. Unable to read it without assistance, he donned, with understated drama, a pair of glasses and noted in an aside: "Gentlemen, you will permit me to put on my spectacles, for I have not only grown gray but almost blind in the service of my country."

An eyewitness to the scene reported that hardened officers wept at the sight. Whether or not we can believe that, such emotional resonance as the spectacle afforded could not have been invoked without the commanding principles observed in the form of the General himself.

[8] For myself (and I take no merit in giving the assurance, being induced to it from principles of gratitude, veracity and justice), a grateful sense of the confidence you have ever placed in me, a recollection of the chearful assistance, and prompt obedience I have experienced from you, under every vicissitude of Fortune, and the sincere affection I feel for an Army, I have so long had the honor to Command, will oblige me to declare, in this public and solemn manner, that, in the attainment of compleat justice for all your toils and dangers, and in the gratification of every wish, so far as may be done consistently with the great duty I owe my Country, and those powers we are bound to respect, you may freely command my Services to the utmost of my abilities.

In this, the penultimate paragraph of the text, Washington cinches the tie. Speaker and audience are now bound in a mutual covenant of faith in the proper order of things, in the essential and binding obligation to respect the superiority of civil over military power. Washington, we observe, is at pains to emphasize the integrity of his motives even as he reaches out toward those of his audience. We accordingly are led to witness a certain play of the self, in which the speaker backgrounds his personal authority—he is animated not by personal interests but by "principles of gratitude, veracity and justice"—in order to foreground the nature of the compact under construction. Seeking the best from his men, he asks for their commitment not to the person of the speaker but to the principles they hold in common. That is why the appropriate gesture here can only be one of gratitude, spurred by affection and the promise to labor on behalf of their legitimate claims on the public trust. The preceding paragraph sought to assure the Newburgh officers that they had reason to believe that Congress would be forthcoming—even if that reason was necessarily a matter of faith. Here Washington cements a bridge between that source of civil authority and the army by asserting through his person the conditions of a promise: he will reward their faith by making good on the covenant, forged through hardship and tempered by a mutual commitment to republican government rightfully conceived.

[9] While I give you these assurances and pledge myself in the most unequivocal manner to exert whatever ability I am possessed of in your favor, let me entreat you, Gentlemen, on your part, not to take any measures which, viewed in the calm light of reason, will lessen the dignity and sully the glory you have hitherto maintained. Let me request you to rely on the plighted faith of your country and place a full confidence in the purity of the intentions of Congress that, previous to dissolution as an army, they will cause all your accounts to be liquidated as directed in their resolutions which were published to you two days ago, and that they will adopt the most effectual measures in their power to render ample justice to you for your faithful and meritorious services. And, let me conjure you in the name of our common country, as you value your own sacred honor, as you respect the rights of humanity, as you regard the military and national character of America, to express your utmost horror and detestation of the man who wishes, under any specious pretenses, to overturn the liberties of our country and who wickedly attempts to open the floodgates of civil discord and deluge our rising empire in blood. By thus determining, and thus acting, you will pursue the plain and direct road to the attainment of your wishes. You will defeat the insidious designs of our enemies, who are compelled to resort from open force to secret artifice. You will give one more distinguished proof of unexampled patriotism and patient virtue, rising superior to the pressure of the most complicated sufferings. And you will, by the dignity of your conduct, afford for posterity to say, when speaking of the glorious example you have exhibited to mankind: "Had this day been wanting, the world had never seen the last stage of perfection to which human nature is capable of attaining.

It was often noted of Washington that he seemed to balance within his very character the conflicting aspirations of his fellow citizens and to so manage the tension as to create something like a perfect equipoise. Underwriting this quality was an unshakable faith in the covenant binding what he would later call "this band of brothers," and it was to them he turned for the final redemption of the crisis. This move is climactic, because through it he invests the officers with the ultimate responsibility to make good on this covenant, to not break faith, and so to make good on their claim to the gratitude of their countrymen. They will be the means through which, by recognizing in Washington the superior claims of moral order, the rightful disposition of civil and military power is restored. All hinges on this act of faith, this ultimate gesture of sacrifice that will bear its won final rewards.

Washington's finest words were all expressed in the form of a charge. Looking ahead to the Circular to the States and to the Inaugural and Farewell Addresses, we see that he possessed a preternatural sense of timing and selected the optimal conditions under which to deliver his most important sentiments. It is characteristic, too, that these charges were designed not so much to impose a moral obligation on a refractory people as to invite them to become what they promised to be. In these, his finest such words, Washington assumed what Thomas Paine assumed in 1776: that Americans had it within themselves to begin the world anew. This would be made possible by a recommitment to a set of ideals that, though now imperiled, stood nevertheless ready to be animated through the resolve of his men. To them he extended the solution to a problem not of their own making, if only they would act according to the terms of the national covenant.

The insurgency has set in dramatic relief the opposed means and ends of revolutionary action; the speaker has offered himself as a beacon in darkened skies; Congress is redeemed; and now—and now it is the officers' glory to resolve the crisis to their greater honor. The recurrent second-person pronouns tell the story and drive home the moral: "you value your own sacred honor, "you respect the rights of humanity," "you regard the military and national character of America," "you will pursue the plain and direct road," "You will defeat the insidious designs of our enemies," "you will give one more distinguished proof of unexampled patriotism and patient virtue," and, in so doing, "you will, by the dignity of your conduct, afford for posterity to say, when speaking of the glorious example you have exhibited to mankind: 'Had this day been wanting, the world had never seen the last stage of perfection to which human nature is capable of attaining.'"

The effect of the speech is thus to drive apart the forces of discord and of moral order, hence to open a space for the interposition of Washington as an exemplar of what he would have his audience become and then to beckon that audience to act accordingly. In the process, Washington has transformed the crisis from a threat into an opportunity. Far from subverting the prospects of republican government, the conspiracy has created the conditions under which the latent virtue of his audience may be realized to optimal ends. One member of that audience recalled "that is happy for America that she has a *patriot army,* and equally so that a *Washington* is its leader." Major Samuel Shaw had seen the General distinguish himself in battle, but on such occasions he had been "supported by the exertions of an army and the countenance of his friends; but in this stood single and alone. . . . Under these circumstances he appeared, not at the head of his troops, but as it were in opposition to them; and for a dreadful moment the interest of the army and its General seemed to be in competition! He spoke—every doubt was dispelled, and the tide of patriotism rolled again in its unwonted course. Illustrious man! What he says of the army may with equal justice be applied to his own character."[18]

Whatever overt resistance that may have lingered in the room was quickly dispelled. Immediately after the speech, General Knox moved for a statement of thanks to the speaker "for his excellent address, and the communication he has been pleased to make to them; and to assure him, that the officers reciprocate his affectionate expressions, with the greatest sincerity of which the human heart is capable." Knox, Colonel Brooks, and Captain Howard were then appointed to draw up a report of the proceedings and return within the hour. The resulting five resolutions made it clear that while Washington's efforts were genuinely appreciated, the concerns that prompted them remained very much at issue. Congress was thus pointedly reminded that from the war's beginning the officers had served "from the purest love, and attachment to the rights and liberties of human nature" and would therefore stand for no policy that would "sully [their] reputation and glory." For all the hardships endured, the officers assured Congress of their abiding faith that "the representatives of America will not disband or disperse the army, until their accounts are liquidated, the balances accurately ascertained, and adequate funds established for payment." The officers then moved that Washington be asked to ask Congress to revisit the petition of late December 1782 and attend to its contents. As for their own state of mind, the Newburgh officers declared that they viewed "with abhorrence, and reject with disdain, the infamous propositions contained in a late anonymous address to the officers of the army, and resent with indignation, the secret attempts by some unknown persons, to collect the officers together, in a manner totally subversive of all discipline and good order." After finally thanking members of the Philadelphia expedition, the assembly moved "that a copy of the proceedings of this day be submitted by the President to Major-General McDougal; and that he be requested to continue his solicitations at Congress, until the objects of his mission are accomplished."

The motions passed individually by unanimous consent under the signature of Major General Horatio Gates.[19]

Washington in the meantime had been communicating the events of the week to Congress, which listened, closely. Madison, among others, was relieved, registering in his notes on the 22nd that "A letter was recd. From Genl Washington inclosing his address to the convention of Officers with the result of their consultations. This dissipation of the cloud which seemed to have been gathering afforded great pleasure on the whole of Congress." Perhaps not the whole of Congress, but enough for most of its members to breathe more easily for the time being. Upon receipt of the General's report, Elias Boudinot immediately responded with a letter to Newburgh. "I duly received your Excellency's letters by the Express," the President of Congress wrote, "containing the proceedings of the Army which gave Congress and every Friend to the Army the highest satisfaction. The commutation of the half pay was passed yesterday," he happily informed Washington, "which adds greatly to our general joy." Those so inclined could now look to the resolution of the crisis as yet further testimony not only to Washington's leadership but to the virtues of the army itself: its "late confusion," noted John Francis Mercer, "has terminated in a manner which reflects additional honor on that band of Patriots."[20]

With news of peace in the air and events reaching a climax, the nationalists' hands were in any case full. Hoping to capitalize on the moment, they moved now to push through half pay. It would not be easy. Eliphet Dyer of Connecticut, for one, was less than impressed by the alleged dangers of a restive army. Its officers, he wrote to Jonathan Trumbull, "have thrown out many Indecent threats, and a proposed Combination forming to carry their points and do themselves Justice as they call it with their Arms and at the Point of the Bayonet threaten not to disband even if Peace is established, but to make themselves a Compleat Compensation by force of Arms, and Judge for themselves." Leaning heavily on the stubborn few who continued to resist the officers' demands, supporters finally persuaded them to rally behind the proposal for half pay. Still mindful of intense New England sentiment against coddling an idle military elite, Dyer nevertheless introduced the motion for half pay on March 20. Two days later, it passed. Such "officers as are now in service," Congress announced, "and shall continue therein to the end of the war, shall be entitled to receive the amount of five years full pay in money or securities, on interest at six per cent per annum, as Congress shall find most convenient, instead of the half pay promised for life, by the resolution of the 21st day of October 1780."[21]

A week later, Washington was able to announce the news in General Orders and on the same day expressed his gratitude to President Elias Boudinot. "The

Commutation of the Half Pay," Washington wrote, "and Measures adopted for the liquidation of their Accounts, will give great satisfaction to the Army; and will prove an additional Tie to strengthen their Confidence in the Justice, and benevolent Intentions of Congress toward them." The General's optimism was shared by many patriots across the new republic, and newspapers quickly picked up the story. A "Farmer" from Pennsylvania recalled that "This step of Congress was at the time universally applauded, and judged to be the political salvation of the country; nor was it esteemed an undue stretch of the prerogative, or a squandering of public monies; but as just, as politic . . . let us own the debt with gratitude," he urged, "and pay it with cheerfulness—let manly motives fire and stimulate our souls—let the world know (should we have occasion for them) that our pay is equal to our promises." This, of course, was the question.[22]

As the weeks and months stretch into summer, it became painfully clear that Congress had not yet secured a firm source of funding for this or any other program of real significance. The nationalist campaign was in fact crumbling before their eyes, the impost was dead, and the officers and army, far from being given "great satisfaction," were growing if anything even more restive. The Pennsylvania Line erupted in June, and though nothing much came of it, the mutiny registered a sour note among the peace festivities. The officers continued to press their Commander to solicit Congress on their behalf, and he obliged them frequently and with force. In time, and in some cases a very long time, the men and officers received some recompense; many did not. By May Washington was directed to begin furloughing the men; by the following month most were gone. It was not a pleasant prospect. "I can assure you," Walter Stewart related to Gates, "had you been a spectator at the scene, your heart would have bled for the poor fellows who were in so disgraceful a manner turned off." Numerous others on the scene testified in similar language, some of it bitter-sweet, some of it seething with resentment. The politics of demobilization are always complex and frequently painful: the disbanding of America's revolutionary forces in the spring and summer of 1783 was no different.[23]

Opponents of the half-pay measure in and out of Congress almost immediately set to work. Most of the arguments recapitulated those aired in 1778 and 1780, hammering hard on concerns about the pretentions of the officer class, equity across the ranks, and undue burdens on taxpaying citizens. Again, New England officials took the lead, knowing their tenure in office was owed to the support of an electorate historically at odds with standing armies and all they portended. Thus the Connecticut *Currant* reported on a town meeting in Torrington, which formally declared its resistance in no uncertain terms: "Why the sufferings of citizen and soldier should be neglected, and all the revenues of the country, be heaped on the officers, is, indeed, a problem difficult to be solved . . . it is an incontestable truth, that some officers left home in low, indigent circumstances, and it is a truth as incontestable that all who return, return in affluence . . . that the most speedy and effectual methods be taken, best calculated to obtain a repeal of those oppressive resolves, and a redress of all grievances." Sentiments like these were given teeth by New England voters, who made their resentments felt by turning out representatives found to have supported the half-pay bill. The whole business, thought Oliver Ellsworth, was a blemish on the new American character. The "clammor" raised "does very illy become a people of sense, especially in the very moment of their salvation, when every heart and voice ought to be joined in praise. But so it is, *Sir,* the princes of power of the air, can raise storms any time when they have occasion for them, having elements to work upon, which, like the raging sea that casteth up mire and dirt, are easily set in motion."[24]

The antipathy made explicit by such opponents can be striking, but it was neither isolated nor unique. For all their genuine faith in the armed forces, the high esteem in which they held the institution, Americans were and remain uneasy about the presence of an army in their midst. The Newburgh crisis moved these anxieties to the front and held them there. Its timing could not have been more poignant, coming as it did after the end and before the beginning. In this liminal zone, the armed forces, its leader, and the American people struggled through to a compromise; like most compromises, it satisfied no one entirely. But the resolution did satisfy enough and as many as necessary to establish above all an attitude. At its core, this attitude was unabashedly idealistic, for in spite of the dire track record of civil-military relations throughout history, Americans have managed for the most part to celebrate *both* arms and polity. They do this, moreover, not in spite of their skepticism about either but because of it. If incessant wrangling over military budgets, jurisdiction, overweening powers, precedents, and constitutional authority is the result, then all the better. That is how ideals are given reality, however bumptious the process. In his own way, but to collective ends, Washington embodied this realization as no other. "We now stand an Independent People," he wrote the Marquis de Lafayette from Newburgh, "and have yet to learn political Tactics. We are placed among the Nations of the Earth, and have a character to establish; but how we shall acquit ourselves time must discover." His handling of the crisis a month earlier suggests that an American "character" was already being forged. Washington had transformed a threat to civilian government into a reconfirmation of civil government. "I shall make no comment on these proceedings," Washington concluded. It was "sufficient to observe, that the more Virtue and forbearance of it [the army] is tried, the more resplendent it appears. My hopes, that the military exit of this valuable class of the community will exhibit such a proof of Amor patria as will do them honor in the page of history." And so it did.[25]

The Newburgh crisis was, as Richard Kohn has written, "significant for what did not happen. No tradition was broken and no experience with direct military intervention occurred to haunt future American political and military life." Why, then, Washington's Newburgh Address and the specific train of events that gave rise to it have not been accorded full-length treatment is not clear. A few considerations suggest themselves. Nineteenth-century historians, good Whigs all, were anxious to stress the glories and the seamless coherence of the quest for independence. No space there for such crises of confidence as beset the heroes. This kind of hagiography gave way in the twentieth century to much greater skepticism about the role of elites generally and to the kind of agency afforded to Great Men, especially great white slave-owning men in uniform. Then, too, scholars of the period have disagreed over details of the episode, and the final version of events probably will never be fully established. But those who have examined it seriously all agree that the Newburgh affair raised issues of the gravest importance.

Conclusion

Any doubts about George Washington's capacity for effective expression ought to be by now dispelled. Although it has not been the aim of this study to defend the General's claim to the status of one of America's great orators, I have sought to position him in a manner to invite reflection on his rhetorical legacy. We are now, at the end of our story of the Newburgh crisis, in a strong position to reassess that legacy and to offer a set of suggestions to that end. Those few who have taken the matter seriously often look to Washington's more heralded productions, notably the Circular to the States, the First Inaugural Address, and the Farewell Address. This is sensible: there they have found prose marked by stringent command of the issues, powerful appeals to the collective good, and political sentiments of enduring value. In the Newburgh Address we are encouraged to witness a figure in dramatically different circumstances, with less time on his hands and pressured by rapidly unfolding events, the outcome of which could not be made certain. The speech of March 15, 1783, was unlike any other he had given or ever would give; at no time in his life was the very fact of his physical presence more decisive, and never was a speech rather than a written document more necessary. This is Washington, the orator. And if his assumption of the role was singular in almost every way, it is no less and perhaps all the more telling for that fact.

In what did Washington's rhetorical art consist? As I hoped to make clear at the outset, we will not get far in answering the question by imposing standards of eloquence alien to his time and the more immediate conditions within which he was obliged to operate. With few exceptions, gentlemen of Washington's class did not nor were they expected to command the hustings in the way of a demagogue, nor even the rostrum as did Webster, Clay, and Calhoun in a later age. Washington was about as far from a populist as one might imagine, and one looked largely in vain to the legislative assembly for displays of political grandiloquence. The Virginian had learned early that deliberation was to be conducted by other means, among those of a similar caste and mutually committed to the decorous process of discussion, compromise, and consensus. Even among such familiar and civil company, Washington was inclined to reticence: self-conscious about his limitations, he sat quietly, listened, and learned. He was not bookish;

he did not wield a graceful pen; he never enjoyed public speaking for its own sake. But along the way he observed how men may be moved, how power works among those who have it, and what it is that can motivate such men to be and to act according to convictions at risk.

Systematic thought about the art of rhetoric reaches back more than two millennia. Its rich bounty of principles and practices offers us much for coming to terms with Washington as a public speaker. Certain features of that lore are clearly germane to our subject, not least its recognition that language is power, its abiding faith in the interinanimation of speech and civic life, its insistence on the potential for individuals to make a difference in public affairs. The age in which Washington lived was in fact enjoying a renaissance of interest in the art generally and in its neoclassical extensions in particular. Hugh Blair, James Burgh, and soon John Quincy Adams, among others, would do much to shape rhetorical education and the scholarly treatment of speech in the forum, at the bar, and in the pulpit. It is nevertheless doubtful that Washington ever read a word of this literature, nor would he have found it of much use even if he had. Despite his many years as a representative to the House of Burgesses and his two terms as chief executive, Washington was not by inclination or talent a political animal, at least in the conventional sense of that term. Unlike so many of his fellow Founders, he seems never to have been interested in the law as a career, and the pulpit, needless to say, did not feature as a fit object of his public aspirations.

Washington, if he was anything, was a soldier. And this fact, so starkly put, explains why standard appeals to the tradition will avail us meager results in seeking to account for Washington's rhetorical legacy. That tradition, interestingly, has remarkably little to say about things military, the more so when we consider the long and benighted presence of war in Western culture. If any headway is to be made toward the project of claiming Washington as a key figure in the gallery of American speakers, this fact needs some explaining of its own. We have noted that its advocates have always posited an intimate relationship between rhetoric and civic life; it stands to reason, then, that they would be largely silent about those practices and institutions, such as the military, that by their nature threaten to usurp the power native to the public sphere. But it is in just this unpromising zone of conflicting forces that the lessons of Washington at Newburgh become most illuminating. The paradox inherent in that crisis is that it provided the speaker an ideal opportunity to reassert the primacy of civic power at precisely the moment when it was most under threat. Thus the claim that Washington was above all a soldier is not as outrageous as it may appear: his achievement was to understand that it was just because he was a soldier of a special kind—a *republican* soldier—that he was responsible for the subordination of military power to civilian. This realization, in turn, required that the moral order undergirding republican principles be given its optimal expression. In the following, I offer a brief set of suggestions as to how we might better understand this achievement—not by ignoring the rhetorical tradition but by applying it more specifically to Washington's singular efforts.

PRACTICAL INTELLIGENCE

Aristotle long ago described the rhetorically adept as possessing the faculty for observing in any given case the available means of persuasion. This seemingly simple construction is in truth loaded with instruction, not least because it stresses the trained capacity for discerning within one's immediate context what one may avail oneself of to meet its distinctive exigencies. A mind so equipped will be highly responsive the here-and-now of a given situation, will understand which kind of appeals are necessary and at hand. The speaker thus mindful is less bound to the rules or systems of the art than to the flexible demands of the moment. The Greek term for this is *phronesis,* a kind of practical intelligence by its nature and function bent toward tactical improvisation. Aristotle thus observes in the *Ethics* that one who is possessed of this virtue is able to deliberate well about the common good, the contingent and practical affairs of shared concern. Pericles and those possessed of his virtues, for example, he deems "prudent" because "they can envisage what is good for themselves and for people in general; we consider that this quality belongs to those who understand the management of households or states." Rhetorical action conceived and executed in this way is essentially a performance art, unfettered by rigid precept or convention and hence free to maximize the givens of the situation. Because the grounds upon which persuasion operates are so often shifting and the contingencies so many and often uncertain, just this kind of intelligence, among all others, is crucial to rhetorical success.[1]

Earlier in our study mention was made of Washington's "Fabian" approach to battle and a rough analogy applied to his efforts at Newburgh. The point may be sharpened a bit by observing the striking similarities that may be seen at work between the arts of generalship and those of rhetorical practice. To illustrate: in 1939, then Colonel George C. Marshall oversaw the publication of *Infantry in Battle,* a brief manual of sorts designed to establish the basic tenets of military decision making. As a means of highlighting the parallels, the reader might substitute the word "rhetoric" and its cognate senses for "war" in the following passage:

> The art of war has not traffic with rules, for the infinitely varied circumstances and conditions of combat never produces the same situation twice. . . . To master his difficult art he must learn to cut to the heart of a situation, recognize its decisive elements and base his

course of action on these. The ability to do this is not God-given, nor can it be acquired overnight; it is a process of years. He must realize that training in solving problems of all types, long practice in making clear, unequivocal decisions, the habit of concentrating on the question at hand, and an elasticity of mind, are indispensable requisites for the successful practice of war.[2]

Cicero could not have put it better. In its stress on flexibility and discipline, ingenuity and experience, habit and improvisation, Marshall's advice reads as a nearly perfect prescription for rhetorical practice in general and as a representation of Washington's craft in particular. As both leaders knew all too well, this orientation to the respective arts of persuasion and war offers no guarantee: improvisation by its nature carries with it the risk of failure, and Washington knew failure often enough. Historians have commented nevertheless on his capacity for learning through such struggles, and it is worth noting that in the process he never had recourse to fixed plans or unquestioned orthodoxies. Self-confident from the beginning, Washington seems always to have trusted in his own abilities to figure himself into and out of conflict. When he stumbled, as at Fort Necessity, and at Forts Washington and Lee, and at Brandywine, he regrouped, reconsidered, and forged ahead. From war's beginning to end, Washington understood full well that he operated from a position of relative weakness—in mass, in army, in experience, and in training. Excepting Yorktown, the prospects of a major confrontation between both armies on the field therefore had to remain, however begrudgingly, a fantasy. Harassing the flanks, the quick assault and retreat, the ambush and siege: those were the realities, and the result was victory.

The kind of practical wisdom we have seen at work during the Newburgh crisis suggests a strong comparison with the soldier's art of maneuver. It may plausibly be objected that Washington was operating at Newburgh from a relatively strong position; in most ways, yes. But at that point in the war, given the state of the officers and the army and the uncertainties ahead, we must not exaggerate that strength. In any case, it is worth reminding ourselves that the General had options—if not as drastic as Scipio's, they very well might have included courts-martial, formal inquiry, or a range of punitive measures. Instead, Washington anticipated the situation, observed closely its unfolding, and moved quickly, decisively, and prudently to turn the advantage back. That is practical wisdom on the ground, where it belongs.

IDENTIFICATION

Aristotle has taught us much about the status and function of rhetoric as a civic art, and this treatment of Washington's craft remains indebted to the Athenian.

There are certain limitations to his treatment of the subject, however, that must be acknowledged. This is hardly surprising: more than two thousand years is a long shelf life for any theory, much less one devoted to a practice in its nature protean and complex. In seeking to establish the legitimacy of rhetoric as a fit object of philosophical study, Aristotle invested it with a conspicuously rational bias: rhetoric, that is, was best understood as perforce a reason-giving activity, through which persuasion was to be effected by marshalling the most compelling arguments on behalf of a given thesis. This bias had its purpose and served the art of rhetoric well by giving it a sound basis in warrantable claims and by stressing the inferential processes through which people may come to conviction.

Left at that, however, students of the subjects are at a lost to explain how we come to believe and act in ways not reducible to reason making. Experience tells us that humans are if anything especially liable to inducement through all kinds of appeals, that indeed being persuaded through by rational arguments might represent an exception rather than a rule of human behavior. Not until much, much later did students of rhetoric entertain seriously the possibility that in order to account for this fact, we needed to break away from Aristotle's rationalism and invent new vocabularies for the study of rhetoric. Among those who have contributed materially to this revision is Kenneth Burke, an American critic of the twentieth century. Burke boldly proposed that we extend our thinking beyond persuasion as a kind of conversion-through-reasons to a more subtle and illuminating process. He had in mind the manifold ways in which people come together as one—not in defiance of reasons, necessarily, but through a distinctive process of shared aspiration. The term he gives to this process is "identification." "You persuade a man," Burke wrote, "only insofar as you can talk his language by speech, gesture, tonality, order, image, attitude, idea, identifying your ways with his." Burke remains a notoriously elusive thinker, and no effort here is made to unpack the nuances of his insight. But we can take a long step toward understanding Washington's address at Newburgh by reflecting on the point.[3]

That speech, as we have seen, features reasons aplenty, but we will have missed its particular rhetorical force if we ignore the manner in which it enlists the audience in a shared vocabulary wherein all relevant parties are enabled, so to speak, to make sense of themselves. Burke advances this insight about the work of identification by stressing its dialectical character: it is, he writes, "affirmed with earnestness precisely because there is division. Identification is compensatory to division. If men were not apart from one another, there would be no need to proclaim their unity." Identification, that is, makes no sense without division; it thus follows that a speaker who wishes to cement the audience's convictions with his of her own must devote no small amount of labor in constructing a "they" to highlight the imperative of the "we."[4]

A moment's retrospection will make clear how central this process is to the rhetorical force of the Newburgh Address. Indeed, it is not otherwise intelligible. But to stress the work of identification in this context is to immediately confront difficulties. It is not self-evident, for example, that Washington commanded the kind of personality others found especially inviting. Historians relish stories of the icy stare, the rare but startling rage, and the excruciating parlor soirees. All this is true; and while I have sought throughout to free Washington from the marble and cast of posterity, there can be no gainsaying that he was "the aloof American." But, while true, it is also beside the point. Washington's singular rhetorical genius, the Newburgh Address shows us, was to offer himself up as an exemplar without self-regard. There is paradox in this as well, but it is resolved when we recognize the republican ideal thus instantiated. The charismatic speaker and the demagogue succeed when they become ends unto themselves. Washington the republican succeeds because he has become a compelling means to ends greater than himself. And he does this, as Burke suggests, by speaking the language of his listeners, by becoming one with them in a shared commitment to the "glorious cause."

CHARACTER

Rhetorically speaking, there is no such thing as "character," if we mean by that elusive term a set of fixed or inherent attributes of the self. This claim will seem eccentric to certain traditions of thought, including but not limited to Christian ideology, which stress a largely interiorized and private conception of the agent as one who possesses or may possess something akin to virtue. In this view, one may be said to "have" character in a manner independent of its contexts: a person is good—or not—regardless of worldly circumstances or whether or not it is given notice. As a case study in what we might call the politics of character, this book has rather flipped the analysis. Character was for Washington an available means of persuasion, a resource of the self that was to be mobilized in the service of getting things done in an uncertain world by moving others to believe and act in prescribed ways. To speak of his character, then, is to speak of a definitively rhetorical quality, marked by contingency and motive in the realm of the symbolic.

We have noted that Aristotle was concerned to formulate a definition of rhetoric as a kind of reason-giving activity. This stance early in his treatise leads him to consider the sources of reasons appropriate to the art: among these, he stipulates those that are in a sense external to the speaker—that is, already-existing facts, testimony, documents, and so on that may be employed on an as-needed basis—and those that inhere in the person *as a person*. These he terms "artistic," in the sense that they are susceptible to strategic management and are appropriate for the purposes of invention. Thus, character, or "ethos," is taken to be a resource native to one's humanity and, potentially at least, a powerful means of persuasion.[5]

The idea is at once commonsensical and rich with implication. To make it work for us as a means of grasping Washington's own rhetorical art, however, some qualifications are in order. First, Aristotle's treatment of character as an explicitly rhetorical principle came amid fundamental transformations in the role of elites in Athenian civic society. Newly enfranchised citizens, without benefit of entrenched authority, needed to rethink ways of making oneself heard and believed—on the spot. Clearly, we are dealing with a quite different set of dynamics in the case of Washington. Second, there is a strongly instrumental bias in Aristotle's account and that in turn has exerted a very strong influence on the subject ever since. By conceiving of character as a form of proof, we are apt, perhaps too quickly, to downplay the less obvious sense in which it functions as a site of display and of witness. These functions, I have suggested, are integral to Washington's performance at Newburgh. Finally, we must remain mindful that whereas Aristotle and his students sought to locate the civic status and function of ethos, our subject is to be found not in the forum or court or on the street corner but in a military encampment.

A great deal has been written about the character of George Washington, and indeed this book may be read as a variation on the theme. Without rehearsing its many refrains, we might with profit identify at least a brief set of implications suggested by the study. Certain of these are by now almost givens in the Washington scholarship: he was acutely aware of the importance of character in virtually all aspects of life; he labored until the end to cultivate and maintain a desired sense of himself and was willing to go to great lengths to secure it; he understood in some basic sense that character mattered most when it was disclosed in action and thereby made apparent to others as a standard of emulation. At a general level, this extraordinary attention to the rhetorical effect of one's self at once helps us to grasp the effect he had on others. No other American, safe to say, spurred as many and as fulsome testimonies to what such a character may accomplish. Thus Henry Lee:

> Moving in his own orbit, he imparted heat and light to his most distant
> satellites; and combining the physical and moral force of all within his
> sphere, with irresistible weight he took his course, commiserating folly,
> disdaining vice, dismaying treason, and invigorating despondency; until

the auspicious hour arrived, when, united with the intrepid forces of a potent and magnanimous ally, he brought to submission the since conqueror of India; thus finishing his long career of military glory with a luster corresponding to his great name, and, in this his last act of war, affixing the seal of fate to our nation's birth.[6]

Such paeans could be and were repeated throughout the land on the occasion of Washington's death, in 1799. While florid and patterned to the style of the day, these testimonies ought not to be taken lightly or dismissed outright; it says something important about a person when a nation is thus moved. But our task here is to drive the point toward a more specific understanding of how Washington's character functioned to rhetorical ends. The Newburgh crisis, I have argued, gives us a rich opportunity to see up close just this process. In order to take us a few steps closer, we might consider from a different angle what his speech resolving that crisis can tell us about Washington and the work of character. To this end, I will call in the assistance of Edwin Black, a rhetorical critic much interested in the provenance of judgment in rhetorical criticism. "The critic," Black writes, "can see in the auditor implied by a discourse a model of what the rhetor would have his real auditor become. What the critic can find projected by the discourse is the image of a man, and though that man may never find actual embodiment, it is still a man that the image is of." The insight is provocative for the way it encourages us think about how speakers construct not only themselves through the rhetorical act but also idealized images of the audiences to whom they speak. The image so rendered he termed the "second persona." The occasion of Washington's Newburgh Address in turn prompts us to ask how the speaker and his audience—implied and actual—collaborated in resolving the crisis and secured the ends of independence. The analysis has been designed to show that Washington's art lay in his ability to so construct himself that he could be both an object of emulation and an agent of the greater good. He did this not by assuming the office of a prophet, nor by exercising the weapons of the demagogue or the charismatic, nor through appeals to the officers' fear, hatred, greed, or resentment. He did it by reauthorizing an ideal in which they all claimed faith, by giving to that ideal its most compelling aspect, and by inviting his men to become what they had hoped to be through its promise.[7]

DRAMA

In 1956 the famed historian David Herbert Donald published a brief volume under the title *Lincoln Reconsidered: Essays on the Civil War Era*. Its novelty lay in the startling argument that Lincoln was not only a statesman of the first order but also an astute and calculating strategist. It is difficult now to imagine a time when a public figure of Lincoln's stature could be conceived as anything other than the political animal he was, when the machinations required to attain and keep power were thought somehow to reside beneath great leaders. Something of the same might be observed of Washington, whose ambition and affinity for power are now widely recognized. Still, it remains all too tempting to regard the Virginian as dwelling somewhere above the trodden ways, where, through sheer force of character, he was able to reach the heights of leadership, there to lift all others to his station. The story of the Newburgh crisis, as indeed the story of Washington's life, teaches us in no uncertain terms that this is fantasy: His Excellency was in fact a master operative, savvy about the ways of power and people and capable of charting complex routes to his preferred ends.

All great leaders understand that power is the product of design. That is why Washington, among the few others of his rank, expended so much time and energy in ordering the world around him. A look into his General Orders gives exhaustive proof of this habit, whether in scolding the men for not keeping the latrines properly or in announcing the Dauphin's birthday. When affairs took on a degree of importance and urgency, Washington displayed a genius for the arts of dramaturgy, staging episodes and conflict within a theater of his own making. We have mentioned several instances of this art, including his gift for introductions, leave-taking, and rituals of rebirth. We have noted, too, that such moments are most suggestive of Washington's leadership when the stakes were highest, when both past and present pressed hard on decisions made in a critical present. The Newburgh crisis offers us a case study, then, in the theatrics of power and in Washington's capacity for expert direction.

Does this make Washington something less than, well, Washington? Surely no leader was more sincere in his motives, more genuinely committed to his ideals, or more ready to sacrifice his all on their behalf. He was, above all, *the real American*. To stress the elements of design and stagecraft would seem to somehow undercut the probity of the man himself, to make of him, or at least of his actions, something less than real. Such skepticism is fair and needs to be addressed, if only because it bears so closely on our efforts to grasp the rhetorical legacy of our subject. Behind it rests a tradition of thinking about the epistemological and moral status of both drama and rhetoric that dates back at least to Plato. Both arts by their nature reside in the management of appearances: that was Plato's problem, for he saw in both a threat to the superior claims of philosophy and its search for the true and just. But, for all his genius, Plato could not grasp, much less grant, the basic integrity of political life as it plays out in the sublunary realm of human affairs. It was left to his student to imagine otherwise. Aristotle, who of course wrote extensively on both rhetoric and drama, conceived of both arts as basic to what it meant to be human, as forms of expression uniquely suited to individuals living in community with others. By extension, we may see in Washington's leadership in general, and in his Newburgh Address especially, a faculty for discerning the rhetorical potential of drama—and the dramatic potential of rhetoric.

Rhetoric, like drama, does not mask reality. It *is* reality, or at least reality of a kind. Washington understood this at some primal level, as evidenced in his unceasing efforts to spruce up the comportment of the army, his efforts to care for his own dress, and his punctilious attention to the protocols of power. He understood, accordingly, that people are responsive to appearances and that appearances may in turn be managed to ends good or ill. By no means does this necessarily imply that they are thus superficial or somehow antithetical to persistent material realities; on the contrary, as the Newburgh Address makes abundantly clear, Washington comprehended clearly that appearance and reality can be very difficult indeed to distinguish. The challenge, then, was not to subordinate one to the other but to outmaneuver a debased version of circumstances with a better and more compelling image of what might be. The following passage from a letter written to Hamilton in the midst of the unfolding crisis is illustrative of the point. On March 12, Washington confided to his former aid that

> It appears, reports have been propagated in Philadelphia, that dangerous combinations were forming in the Army. . . . From this, and a variety of considerations, it is believed by some, the scheme was not only planned, but also digested and matured in Philadelphia. . . . The matter was managed with great Art. . . . I was obliged therefore, in order to arrest, on the spot, the foot that stood wavering on a tremendous precipice, to prevent the Officers from being taken by surprize while the passions were all inflamed, and to rescue them from plunging themselves into a gulph of Civil horror from which there might be no receding.[8]

Washington, we know, had been informed well in advance that such rumors were afoot; he knew who was likely behind them; and he was fully prepared to meet the inevitable crisis head on. We recall, too, that it was entirely within his power to shut the whole business summarily down. He did not. Events were allowed to unfold, but according now to his own script. Immediately seizing the initiative, Washington in effect hijacked the proceedings, called for a meeting of his own time and place, and unexpectedly showed up at the Temple. There he consummated the crisis through a kind of deus ex machina, not by shaming the officers into submission but by rousing them to a reawakened image of who they were and who they might become. History could not ask for a more dramatic, a more rhetorically opportune performance.

———— • ————

The list of virtues attached to the person of George Washington is long, and his celebrants have not yet tired of rehearsing them more than two centuries after his death. I have sought in this study of the Newburgh crisis not to take up the refrain again but to offer an account of what those qualities look like when put to work in the salvation of republican ideals. Along the way, I have not been reticent in giving Washington his due or in pointing out his limitations. The greater goal has been to provide a reason for revisiting an episode that, while generally well known, remains underappreciated as a key moment in the American revolutionary inheritance. In the end, Washington conducted himself at Newburgh just as we hoped he might: with eloquence of a sort, with moral authority, and with an unwavering commitment to the greater good. That he proved successful may not be surprising, but what he achieved that spring day along the Hudson ought never to be taken for granted. It remains a lodestar for dark times.

APPENDIX A

Memorial from the Officers of the Army

Philadelphia
December, 1782
To the United States in Congress assembled.

The address and petition of the officers of the army of the United States,

Humbly sheweth, that we, the officers of the army of the United States, in behalf of ourselves and our brethren the soldiers, beg leave, with all proper deference and respect, freely to state to Congress, the supreme power of the United States, the great distress under which we labor.

At this period of the war it is with peculiar pain we find ourselves constrained to address your august body, on matters of a pecuniary nature. We have struggled with our difficulties, year after year, under the hopes that each would be the last; but we have been disappointed. We find our embarrassments thicken so fast, and have become so complex, that many of us are unable to go further. In this exigence we apply to Congress for relief as our head and sovereign.

To prove that our hardships are exceedingly disproportionate to those of any other citizens of America, let a recurrence be had to the paymaster's accompts, for four years past. If to this it should be objected, that the respective states have made settlements, and given securities for the pay due, for part of that time, let the present value of those nominal obligations be ascertained by the monied men, and they will be found to be worth little indeed; and yet, trifling as they are, many have been under the sad necessity of parting with them, to prevent their families from actually starving.

We complain that shadows have been offered to us while the substance has been gleaned by others.

Our situation compels us to search for the cause of our extreme poverty. The citizens murmur at the greatness of their taxes, and are astonished that no part reaches the army. The numerous demands, which are between the first collectors and the soldiers, swallow up the whole.

Our distresses are now brought to a point. We have borne all that men can bear—our property is expended—our private resources are at an end, and our friends are wearied out and disgusted with our incessant applications. We, therefore, most seriously and earnestly beg, that a supply of money may be forwarded to the army as soon as possible. The uneasiness of the soldiers, for want of pay, is great and dangerous; any further experiments on their patience may have fatal effects.

The promised subsistence or ration of provisions consisted of certain articles specified in kind and quantity. This ration, without regard, that we can conceive, to the health of the troops, has been frequently altered, as necessity or conveniency suggested, generally losing by the change some part of its substance. On an average, not more than seven or eight-tenths have been issued; the retained parts were, for a short time, paid for; but the business became troublesome to those who were to execute it. For this, or some other reasons, all regard to the dues, as they respected the soldiers, has been discontinued (now and then a trifling gratuity excepted). As these dues respected the officers, they were compensated, during one year and part of another, by an extra ration; as to the retained rations, the account for several years remains unsettled; there is a large balance due upon it, and a considerable sum for that of forage.

The clothing was another part of the soldier's hire. The arrearages on that score, for the year 1777, were paid off in continental money, when the dollar was worth about four-pence; the arrearages for the following years are unliquidated, and we apprehend scarcely thought of but by the army. Whenever there has been a real want of means, any defect in system, or neglect in execution, in the departments of the army, we have invariably been the sufferers, by hunger and nakedness, and by languishing in an hospital.

We beg leave to urge an immediate adjustment of all dues; that as great a part as possible be paid, and the remainder put on such a footing as will restore cheerfulness to the army, revive confidence in the justice and generosity of its constituents, and contribute to the very desirable effect of re-establishing public credit.

We are grieved to find that our brethren, who retired from service on half-pay, under the resolution of Congress in 1780, are not only destitute of any effectual provision, but are become the objects of obloquy. Their condition has a very discouraging aspect on us who must sooner or later retire, and from every consideration of justice, gratitude and policy, demands attention and redress.

We regard the act of Congress respecting half-pay, as an honorable and just recompense for several years hard service, in which the health and fortunes of the officers have been worn down and exhausted. We see with chagrin the odious point of view in which the citizens of too many of the states endeavor to place the men entitled to it. We hope, for the honor of human nature, that there are none so hardened in the sin of ingratitude, as to deny the justice of the reward. We have reason to believe that the objection generally is against the mode only. To prevent therefore, any altercations and distinctions which may tend to injure that harmony which we ardently desire may reign throughout the community, we are willing to commute the half-pay pledged, for full pay for a certain number of years, or for a sum in gross, as shall be agreed to by the committee sent with this address. And in this we pray, that the disabled officers and soldiers, with the widows and orphans of those who have expended or may expend their lives in the service of their country, may be fully comprehended. We also beg, that some mode may be pointed out for the eventual payment of those soldiers who are the subjects of the resolution of Congress of the 15th May, 1778.

To the representation now made, the army have not a doubt that Congress will pay all that attention which the serious nature of it requires. It would be criminal in the officers to conceal the general dissatisfaction which prevails, and is gaining ground in the army, from the pressure of evils and injuries, which, in the course of seven long years, have made their condition in many instances wretched. They therefore entreat, that Congress, to convince the army and the world that the independence of America shall not be placed on the ruin of any particular class of her citizens, will point out a mode for immediate redress.

APPENDIX B

The Newburgh Circulars

10 March, 1783.

A Meeting of the Genl & Field Officers is requested, at the public Building, on Tuesday next, at 11 oClock—A Commissd Officer from each Company is expected, and a Delegate from the Medical Staff—The Object of this Convention, is to consider the late Letter from our Representatives in Philadelphia; and what measures (if any) should be adopted, to obtain that redress of Grievances, which they seem to have solicited in vain.

THE FIRST ANONYMOUS LETTER

10 March, 1983.

Gentlemen,

A fellow soldier whose interests and affections bind him strongly to you, whose past sufferings, have been as great & whose future fortune may be as desperate as yours, would beg leave to address you.

Age has its claims, and rank is not without its pretensions to advise—but tho unsupported by both, he flatters himself that the plain language of sincerity & Experience will neither be unheard nor unregarded.

Like many of you he loved private life, and left it with regret—he left it determined to retire from the field with the necessity that called him to it, and not till then, Not, 'till the enemies of his Country, the slaves of pow'r and the hirelings of injustice were compelled to abandon their schemes, and acknowledge America as terrible in Arms, as she had been humble in Remonstrance—with this object in view, he has long shared in your Toils and mingled in your dangers. He has felt the cold hand of poverty without a murmur, & has seen the insolence of wealth without a sigh. But, too much under the direction of his wishes, and sometimes weak enough to mistake desire for opinion, he has till lately, very lately believed in the Justice of his Country. He hop'd, that, as the Clouds of adversity scattered, and as the sunshine of peace & better fortune broke in upon us, the coldness and severity of government would relax, and that more than Justice, that gratitude, would blaze forth upon those hands, which had upheld her in the darkest stages of her passage from impending servitude to Acknowledged Independence, But faith has its limits as well as Temper—and there are points beyond which neither can be streched, without sinking into Cowardice or plunging into credulity. This, my friends, I conceive to be your situation—hurried to the very verge of both—another step would ruin you forever—To be tame and unprovoked when injuries press hard upon you, is more than weakness, but to look up for Kinder usage, without one manly Effort of your own, would fix your Character & shew the world how richly you deserve those Chains you broke—To guard against this evil, let us take a review of the ground upon which we now stand, and from thence carry our thoughts forward for a moment, into the unexplored field of expedient.

After a pursuit of seven long Years, the object for which we set out, is at length brot within our reach—Yes, my friends, that suffering Courage of yours, was active once, it has conducted the United States of America, thro' a doubtfull and a bloody War—it has placed her in the Chair of Independancy—and peace returns again to bless—Whom?—a Country willing to redress your wrongs? cherrish your worth—and reward your Services—a Country courting your return to private life, with Tears of gratitude & smiles of Admiration—longing to divide with you, that Independancy, which your Gallantry has given, and those riches which your wounds have preserved. Is this the case? or is it rather a Country that tramples upon your rights, disdains your Cries—& insults your distresses? have you not more than once suggested your wishes—and made known your wants to Congress (wants and wishes, which gratitude and policy should have anticipated, rather than evaded)—and have you not lately, in the meek language of intreating Memorials, begged from their Justice, what you would no longer expect from their favor. How have you been answered? let the letter which you are called to consider tomorrow, make reply. If this then be your treatment while the swords you wear are necessary for the Defence of America, what have you to expect from peace; when your voice shall sink, and your strength dissipate by division—when those very swords, the Instruments and Companions of your Glory, shall be taken from your sides, and no remaining mark of Military distinction left, but your wants, infirmities & Tears—can you then consent to be the only sufferers by this revolution—and retiring from the field, grow old in poverty, wretchedness, and Contempt; can you consent, to wade thro' the vile mire of dependency, and owe the miserable remnant of that life to Charity, which has hitherto been spent in honor? If you can—Go—and carry with you the jest of Tories, & the Scorn of Whigs—the ridicule—and what is worse—the pity of the world—go—Starve and be forgotten. But if your spirits should revolt at this—if you have sense enough to discover, and spirit enough to oppose tyranny, under whatever Garb it may assume—whether it be the plain Coat of Republicanism—or the splendid Robe of Royalty—if you have yet learned to discriminate between a people and a Cause—between men & principles—Awake—attend to your Situation & redress yourselves; If the present moment be lost, every future Effort, is in vain—and your threats then, will be as empty, as your entreaties now—I would advise you therefore, to come to some final opinion, upon what you can bear—and what you will suffer—If your determination be in any proportion to your wrongs—carry your appeal from the Justice to the fears of government—Change the Milk & Water stile of your last Memorial—assume a bolder Tone, decent, but lively, spirited and determined—And suspect the man, who would advise to more moderation, and longer forbearance. Let two or three Men, who can feel as well as write, be appointed to draw up your last Remonstrance (for I would no longer give it the sueing, soft, unsuccessfull Epithet of Memorial). Let it be represented in language that will neither dishonor you by its Rudeness, nor betray you by its fears—what has been promised by Congress and what has been performed—how long and how patiently you have suffered—how little you have asked, and how much of that little, have been denied—Tell them, that tho' you were the first, and would wish to be the last to encounter Danger—tho' dispair itself can never drive you into dishonor, it may drive you from the field—That the wound often irritated and never healed, may at length become incurable—and that the slightest mark of indignity from Congress now, must operate like the Grave, and part you forever—That in any political Event, the Army has its alternative—If peace, that nothing shall seperate them from your Arms but Death—If War—that courting the Auspicies, and inviting the direction of your Illustrous Leader, you will retire to some unsettled Country, Smile in your Turn, and "mock when their fear cometh on"—But let it represent also, that should they comply with the request of your late Memorial, it would make you more happy; and them more respectable—That while War should continue, you would follow their standard into the field, and When it came to an End, you would withdraw into the shade of private Life—and give the World another subject of Wonder & applause—An Army victorious over its Enemies, Victorious over itself.

THE SECOND ANONYMOUS LETTER

12 March 1783

Gentlemen

The Author of a late Address, anxious to deserve, 'tho he should fail to Engage your Esteem, and determined, at every risque, to unfold your duty, &

discharge his own—would beg leave to solicit this further Indulgence of a few moments attention.

Aware of the Coyness with which his last letter would be received; he feels himself neither disappointed; nor displeased with the caution it has met—Ye well knew that it spoke a Language, which 'till now had been heard only in whispers, and that it contained some sentiments, which confidence itself would have breathed with distrust. But, their Lives have been short indeed, and their Observations imperfect indeed, who have yet to learn, that alarms may be false—that the best designs are sometimes obliged to assume the worst Aspects, and that however synonimous Surprize & disaster may be in military phrase—in moral & political meaning, they convey Ideas, as different as they are distinct.

Suspicion, detestable as it is in private Life, is the loveliest trait of political Characters—It prompts you to enquiry—bars the Door against Designs, and opens every Avenue to truth—It was the first to oppose a Tyrant here, and still stands centinel over the Liberties of America—With this Belief, it would illy become me, to stifle the Voice of this honest Guardian—a guardian, who, (authorized by circumstances, digested into proof) has herself given Birth to the Address you have read, and now goes forth among you, with a request to all, that it may be treated fairly—that it may be considered before it be abused—and condemned, before it be tortured, convinced that in a search after Error, Truth will appear—that apathy itself will grow warm in the pursuit, and tho' it will be the last to adopt her advice, it will be the first to act upon it.

The General Orders of Yesterday which the weak may mistake for disapprobation, and the designing dare to represent as such, wears, in my opinion, a very different complexion, and carries with it a very opposite tendency—Till now, the Commandr in Chief has regarded the Steps you have taken for redress, with good wishes alone. Tho' ostensible Silence has authorised your meetings and his private Opinion has sanctified your Claims—Had he disliked the Object in view would not the same sense of Duty which forbad you from meeting on the third Day of this Week, have forbidden you from meeting on the seventh? Is not the same subject held up for your discussion, and has it not passed the seal of office, and taken all the solemnity of an Order—this will give system to your proceedings, and stability to your resolves, will ripen speculation into fact, and while it adds to the unanimity, it cannot possibly lessen the Independency of your sentiments—It may be necessary to add upon this subject, that from the Injunction with which the general Orders close, every man is at Liberty to conclude that the Report, to be made to Head Quarters, is intended for Congress—Hence will arise another motive for that Energy, which has been recommended—for can you give the lie to the pathetic discriptions of your representations & the more alarming predictions of our friends?

To such as make a Want of signature an objection to opinion, I reply—that it matters very little who is the Author of Sentiments which grow out of your feelings, and apply to your Wants—That in this Instance Diffidence suggested what Experience enjoins, and that while I continue to move on the high road of Argument and Advice, (which is open to all) I shall continue to be the sole Confident of my own secret—But should the Time come, when it shall be necessary to depart from this general line, and hold up any Individual among you, as an Object of the resentment or contempt of the rest, I thus publicly pledge my Honor as a soldier, and veracity as a Man, that I will then assume a visible existence, and give my name to the Army, with as little reserve as I now give my Opinions. I am &c.

APPENDIX C

George Washington's Speech at Newburgh

Saturday, March 15, 1783

By an anonymous summons, an attempt has been made to convene you together. How inconsistent with the rules of propriety, how unmilitary and how subversive of all order and discipline let the good sense of the army decide.

In the moment of this summons, another anonymous production was sent into circulation, addressed more to the feelings of passions than to the reason and judgment of the army. The author of the piece is entitled to much credit for the goodness of his pen, and I could wish he had as much credit for the rectitude of his heart. For, as men, we see through different optics, and are induced by the reflecting faculties of the mind to use different means to attain the same end. The author of the address should have had more charity than to mark with suspicion the man who would recommend moderation or longer forbearance, or, in other words, who should not think as he thinks and act as he advises. But, he had another plan in view, in which candor and liberality of sentiment, regard for justice, and love of country have no part. And, he was right to insinuate the darkest suspicion to effect the blackest designs.

That the address is drawn with great art and is designed to answer the most insidious purposes, that it is calculated to impress the mind with an idea of premeditated injustice to the sovereign power of the United States and rouse all those resentments which must unavoidably flow from such a belief, that the secret mover of this scheme (whoever he may be) intended to take advantage of the passions while they were warmed by the recollection of past distresses without giving time for cool, deliberative thinking and that composure of mind which is so necessary to give dignity and stability to measures is rendered too obvious by the mode of conducting the business to need other proof than a reference to the preceding.

Thus much, Gentlemen, I have thought it incumbent on me to observe to you, to show upon what principles I opposed the irregular and hasty meeting which was proposed to have been held on Tuesday last, and not because I wanted a disposition to give you every opportunity, consistent with your honor and the dignity of the army, to make known your grievances. If my conduct heretofore has not evinced to you that I have been a faithful friend to the army, my declaration of it at this time would be equally unavailing and improper. But, as I was among the first who embarked in the cause of our common country, as I have never left your side one moment but when called on public duty, as I have been the constant companion and witness of your distresses and not among the last to feel and acknowledge your merits, as I have ever considered my own military reputation as inseparably connected with that of the army, as my heart has ever expanded with joy when I heard its praises and my indignation has arisen when the mouth of detraction has been opened against it, it can scarcely be supposed, at this late stage of the war, that I am indifferent to its interests.

But, how are they to be promoted? The way is plain, says the anonymous addresser. If war continues, remove into the unsettled country, there establish yourselves, and leave an ungrateful country to defend itself. But, who are they to defend? Our wives, our children, our farms, and other property which we leave behind us. Or, in this state of hostile separation, are we to take the first two (the latter cannot be removed) to perish in a wilderness with hunger, cold and nakedness? If peace takes place, never sheath your sword, says he, until you have obtained full and ample justice. This dreadful alternative, of deserting our country in the extremest hour of her distress or turning our arms against it (which is the apparent object unless Congress can be compelled into instant compliance) has something so shocking in it that humanity revolts at the idea. My God! What can this writer have in view by recommending such measures? Can he be a friend to the army? Can he be a friend to this country? Rather is he not an insidious foe, some emissary, perhaps, from New York, plotting the ruin of both by sowing the seeds of discord and separation between the civil and military powers of the continent? And, what compliment does he pay to our understandings when he recommends measures in either alternative impracticable in their nature?

But here, Gentlemen, I will drop the curtain. And, because it would be as imprudent in me to assign my reasons for this opinion as it would be insulting to your conception to suppose you stood in need of them, a moment's reflection will convince every dispassionate mind of the physical impossibility of carrying either proposal into execution.

There might, Gentlemen, be an impropriety in my taking notice in this address to you of an anonymous production, but the manner in which that performance has been introduced to the army, the effect it was intended to have, together with some other circumstances, will amply justify my observations on the

tendency of that writing. With respect to the advice given by the author to suspect the man who shall recommend moderate measures and longer forbearance
—I spurn it, as every man who regards that liberty and reveres that justice for
which we contend undoubtedly must. For if men are to be precluded from offering their sentiments on a matter which may involve the most serious and alarming consequences that can invite the consideration of mankind, reason is of no
use to us. The freedom of speech may be taken away and, dumb and silent, we
may be led like sheep to the slaughter.

I cannot, in justice to my own belief and what I have great reason to conceive is the intention of Congress, conclude this address without giving it as my
decided opinion that that Honorable body entertain exalted sentiments of the
services of the army and, from a full conviction of its merits and sufferings, will
do it complete justice. That their endeavors to discover and establish funds for
this purpose have been unwearied and will not cease till they have succeeded,
I have no doubt. But, like all other large bodies where there is a variety of different interests to reconcile, their deliberations are slow. Why then should we
distrust them and, in consequence of that distrust, adopt measures which may
cast a shadow over that glory which has been so justly acquired and tarnish the
reputation of an army which is celebrated through all Europe for its fortitude and
patriotism? And for what is this done? To bring the object we seek nearer? No!
Most certainly, in my opinion, it will cast it at a greater distance.

For myself (and I take no merit in giving the assurance, being induced to it
from principles of gratitude, veracity and justice), a grateful sense of the confidence you have ever placed in me, a recollection of the cheerful assistance and
prompt obedience I have experienced from you under every vicissitude of fortune, and the sincere affection I feel for an army I have so long had the honor to
command, will oblige me to declare in this public and solemn manner that in the
attainment of complete justice for all your toils and dangers and in the gratification of every wish, so far as may be done consistently with the great duty I owe
my country and those powers we are bound to respect, you may freely command
my services to the utmost of my abilities.

While I give you these assurances and pledge myself in the most unequivocal
manner to exert whatever ability I am possessed of in your favor, let me entreat
you, Gentlemen, on your part, not to take any measures which, viewed in the
calm light of reason, will lessen the dignity and sully the glory you have hitherto
maintained. Let me request you to rely on the plighted faith of your country and
place a full confidence in the purity of the intentions of Congress that, previous
to dissolution as an army, they will cause all your accounts to be liquidated as
directed in their resolutions which were published to you two days ago, and that

they will adopt the most effectual measures in their power to render ample justice to you for your faithful and meritorious services. And, let me conjure you in the name of our common country, as you value your own sacred honor, as you respect the rights of humanity, as you regard the military and national character of America, to express your utmost horror and detestation of the man who wishes, under any specious pretenses, to overturn the liberties of our country and who wickedly attempts to open the floodgates of civil discord and deluge our rising empire in blood.

By thus determining, and thus acting, you will pursue the plain and direct road to the attainment of your wishes. You will defeat the insidious designs of our enemies, who are compelled to resort from open force to secret artifice. You will give one more distinguished proof of unexampled patriotism and patient virtue, rising superior to the pressure of the most complicated sufferings. And you will, by the dignity of your conduct, afford for posterity to say, when speaking of the glorious example you have exhibited to mankind: "Had this day been wanting, the world had never seen the last stage of perfection to which human nature is capable of attaining."

NOTES

Introduction

1. Washington Irving, "A Chronicle of Wolfert's Roost," in *Wolfert's Roost and Miscellanies* (New York: Century, 1901), 9; Thomas Cole, quoted in *Thomas Cole's Poetry*, ed. Marshall B. Tymn (New York: George Shumway, 1972), 169; William Cullen Bryant, "Scene on the Banks of the Hudson," in Arthur G. Adams, ed., *The Hudson River in Literature* (Albany: SUNY Press, 1980), 219.

2. An informative series of pieces on life at Newburgh appeared in several nineteenth-century periodicals; see J. T. Headley, "Washington's Headquarters at Newburgh," *The Galaxy* 22, no. 1 (1876): 7–21; Russell Headley, "The Old Cantonment at Newburgh," *The New England Magazine* 13, no. 5 (1896): 578–593; and J. T. Headley, "Last Days of Washington's Army at Newburgh," *Harper's New Monthly Magazine* 67 (October 1883): 651–672.

3. George Washington, *The Writings of George Washington from the Original Manuscript Sources 1745–1799, Vol. 26: January 1, 1783–June 10, 1783*, ed. John C. Fitzpatrick (Washington, DC: US Government Printing Office, 1931–44).

4. James Thomas Flexner, *Washington: The Indispensable Man* (New York: Signet, 1984), 177; Joseph J. Ellis, *His Excellency: George Washington* (New York: Knopf, 2004), 142; Richard Norton Smith, *Patriarch: George Washington and the New American Nation* (New York: Houghton Mifflin, 1993), 19; Don Higginbotham, *George Washington and the American Military Tradition* (Athens: University of Georgia Press, 1985), 98.

5. Robert Middlekauff, *The Glorious Cause: The American Revolution, 1763–1789* (New York: Oxford University Press, 1982), 583.

6. John Alden, *George Washington: A Biography* (Baton Rouge: Louisiana State University Press, 1984), xi; Marcus Cunliffe, *George Washington: Man and Monument* (Boston: Little, Brown, 1958), 14; John E. Ferling, *The First of Men: A Life of George Washington* (Knoxville: University of Tennessee Press, 1988), xi.

7. Marquis de Chastellux, *Travels in North America*, trans. W. E. Schenck (New York: White, Gallaher, and White, 1827), 72; Thomas Jefferson, *Writings*, ed. Merrill Peterson (New York: The Library of America, 1984), 1318–1321.

8. *Virginia Gazette*, January 24, 1777, 1; *Providence Gazette*, March 24, 1781, 2.

9. Here I draw largely upon Don Higginbotham, *War of American Independence: Military Attitudes, Policies, and Practices, 1763–1789* (New York: Macmillan, 1971).

10. The standard account of the war's financial travails is still E. James Ferguson, *The Power of the Purse: A History of American Public Finance, 1776–1790* (Chapel Hill: University of North Carolina Press, 1961).

11. Higginbotham, *American Independence*, 289.

12. Knox to Benjamin Lincoln, December 20, 1782, quoted in Mark Puls, *Henry Knox: Visionary General of the American Revolution* (New York: Palgrave Macmillan, 2008), 173; Washington to Theodore Bland, April 4, 1783, *Writings*, 26: 294–95.

13. Albert Furtwangler, *American Silhouettes: Rhetorical Identities of the Founders* (New Haven: Yale University Press, 1987), 64, 97.

14. Flexner, *Indispensable Man*, 178.

15. John Shy, *A People Numerous and Armed: Reflections on the Military Struggle for American Independence* (Ann Arbor: University of Michigan Press, 1990), 236.

16. William Abbott, ed., *Memoirs of Major-General William Heath* (New York: William Abbott, 1901), 337.

17. *Independent Chronicle* [Boston], June 12, 1783, 1; *Boston Evening Post*, August 16, 1783, 1.

18. Jefferson to Washington, April 16, 1784, in Paul H. Smith, ed., *Letters of Delegates to Congress* (Washington, DC: Library of Congress, 1976–2000), 21: 521–524.

19. *Norwich Packet*, April 1, 1784, 2.

20. Washington to Steuben, March 15, 1784, *Papers of George Washington* (Confederation Series), ed. W. W. Abbot (Charlottesville: University of Virginia Press, 1992), 220–221.

21. Elbridge Gerry, June 2, 1784, in Worthington C. Ford et al., eds., *Journals of the Continental Congress, 1774–1789*, 34 vols. (Washington, DC: US Government Printing Office, 1904–37), 27: 518–519.

Chapter 1. Washington's Character and the Craft of Military Leadership

1. On Washington's public and self-fashioning, see especially Cunliffe, *George Washington;* Paul Longmore, *Invention of George Washington* (Berkeley: University of California Press, 1988); John S. Hallam, "Houdon's Washington in Richmond: Some New Observations," *American Art Journal* 10, no. 2 (1978): 72–80; Stuart Leibiger, "'To Judge of Washington's Conduct': Illuminating George Washington's Appearance on the World Stage," *Virginia Magazine of History and Biography* 107, no. 1 (1999): 37–44; Saul Padover, "George Washington—Portrait of a True Conservative," *Social Research* 22, no. 2 (1955): 199–222; Barry Schwartz, *George Washington: The Making of an American Symbol* (New York: Free Press, 1987); and Garry Wills, *Cincinnatus: George Washington and the Enlightenment* (Garden City, NY.: Doubleday, 1984).

2. *Edinbourough Magazine and London Review,* March 1800, 179; for additional treatment of Washington from the British perspective see Troy O. Bickham, "Sympathizing with Sedition? George Washington, the British Press, and British Attitudes during the American War of Independence," *William and Mary Quarterly* 59, no. 1 (2002): 101–122; and Martin Kallich and Andrew Macleish, eds., *American Revolution through British Eyes* (New York: Harper and Row, 1962).

3. Oliver Everett, *An Eulogy, on General George Washington* (Charlestowne, MA: Samuel Etheridge, 1800), 8–9; John B. Johnson, *Eulogy on General Washington* (Albany, NY: L. Andrews, 1800), 14; George Richards Minot, *Eulogy on George Washington* (Boston: Manning and Loring, 1800), 20; Thomas Paine, *On the Life of George Washington* (Newburyport, MA: Edmund M. Blunt, 1800), 56; Richard Henry Lee, *A Funeral Oration* (Philadelphia: John Ormond, 1799), 2.

4. For Washington's strategic sense of self, see in particular Cunliffe, *George Washington,* and Longmore, *Invention of George Washington.*

5. Washington's sense of theatricality is examined in Furtwangler, *American Silhouettes;* Sandra Gustafson, *Eloquence Is Power: Oratory and Performance in Early America* (Chapel Hill: University of North Carolina Press, 2000), 226–232; and Wills, *Cincinnatus,* 6–9.

6. Thomas Paine, *Common Sense,* quoted in Scott Liell, *Forty-Six Pages* (Philadelphia: Running Press, 2003), 204–205; on the philosophical foundations of the era see especially Robert A. Ferguson, *American Enlightenment, 1750–1820* (Cambridge, MA: Harvard University Press, 1997); on Washington's powers of inauguration see Stephen E. Lucas, "Genre Criticism and Historical Context: The Case of George Washington's First Inaugural Address." *The Southern Speech Journal* 51, no. 4 (1986): 354–370.

7. Hannah Arendt, *The Human Condition* (Chicago: University of Chicago Press, 1958), 177.

8. On conceptions of character and its expression, see Andrew Burstein, "The Political Character of Sympathy," *Journal of the Early Republic* 21, no. 4 (2001): 601–632; Alan Taylor, "From Fathers to Friends of the People: Political Personas in the Early Republic," *Journal of the Early Republic* 11, no. 4 (1991): 465–491; and Andrew S. Trees, *The Founding Fathers and the Politics of Character* (Princeton: Princeton University Press, 2004).

9. Walpole, quoted in Peter R. Henriques, *Realistic Visionary: A Portrait of George Washington* (Charlottesville: University of Virginia Press, 2008), 6.

10. Andrew Jackson, *Papers of Andrew Jackson,* ed. Harold D. Mores and J. Clint Cliff (Knoxville: University of Tennessee Press, 2002), 6: 1.

11. Daniel L. Dreisback, "The 'Vine and Fig Tree' in George Washington's Letters: Reflections on a Biblical Motif in the Literature of the American Founding Era," *Anglican and Episcopal History* 76, no. 3 (2007): 299–326.

12. Quoted in Ron Chernow, *Washington: A Life* (New York: Penguin, 2010), 45; Wills, *Cincinnatus,* 3; Ellis, *His Excellency,* 221.

13. Paul Seabury, "Provisionality and Finality," *Annals of the American Academy of Political and Social Science* 392 (November1970): 96–104.

14. Jefferson, in Peterson, *Writings,* 1317.

15. Washington, *Journal* (Williamsburg, VA: William Hunter, 1754), 2. For Washington's early military career, see Alden, *Washington,* 47–72; James Thomas Flexner, *George Washington: The Forge of Experience, 1732–1775* (Boston: Little, Brown, 1965), 59–226.

16. The classic statement on this theme remains Douglas Adair, *Fame and the Founding Fathers* (Indianapolis: Liberty Fund, 1998).

17. Glenn A. Phelps, *George Washington and American Constitutionalism* (Lawrence: University Press of Kansas, 1993).

18. On Jumonville and Fort Necessity, see Flexner, *Forge,* 87–93; 104–106; 99–112.

19. Washington, *Writings,* 1: 20.

20. Higginbotham, *American Military Tradition,* 35; Flexner, *Forge,* 107; Alden, *Washington,* 70.

21. Dinwiddy, in Washington, *Writings,* 1: 106, note 75.

22. Fitzhugh, in Washington, *Writings,* 1: 105, note 72.

23. Washington, *Writings*, 1: 104–105.

24. Orme, in Washington, *Writings*, 1: 110.

25. Washington, *Writings*, 1: 107; 112; 115.

26. Edmund Morgan, "George Washington: The Aloof American," in *George Washington Reconsidered*, ed. Don Higginbotham (Charlottesville: University Press of Virginia, 2001), 295; Flexner, *Forge*, 309.

27. Alden, *Washington*, 1: 94–95.

28. Donald M. Sweig, "A New-Found Washington Letter of 1774 and the Fairfax Resolves," *William and Mary Quarterly* 40, no. 2 (1983): 285.

29. Flexner, *Forge*, 316; Washington, *Writings*, 1: 227.

30. On conspiracy as a theme in revolutionary discourse, see Stephen E. Lucas, *Portents of Rebellion: Rhetoric and Revolution in Philadelphia, 1765–76* (Philadelphia: Temple University Press, 1976); and Gordon Wood, "Conspiracy and the Paranoid Style: Causality and Deceit in the Eighteenth Century," *William and Mary Quarterly* 39, no. 3 (1982): 401–441.

31. Washington, *Writings*, 1: 228–2289; 231; 232; 242.

32. Flexner, *Forge*, 315; Washington, *Writings*, 1: 232–233; 234.

33. Washington, *Writings*, 1: 240–241.

34. The most authoritative treatment of the winter's ordeal is Wayne Bodle, *The Valley Forge Winter: Civilians and Soldiers in War* (University Park: Pennsylvania State University Press, 2002).

35. For camp conditions see Bodle, *Valley Forge Winter*; E. Wayne Carp, *To Starve the Army at Pleasure* (Chapel Hill: University of North Carolina Press, 1984); and Caroline Cox, *A Proper Sense of Honor: Service and Sacrifice in George Washington's Army* (Chapel Hill: University of North Carolina Press, 2004).

36. Washington, General Orders, in *Writings*, 10: 167–168.

37. Henry Dearborn, *Revolutionary War Journals of Henry Dearborn*, ed. Lloyd A. Brown and Howard H. Peckham (Chicago: Caxton Club, 1939), 118.

38. Washington, *Writings*, 10: 192; 209; 425.

39. *Continental Journal* [Boston], January 29, 1778, 2; *New Jersey Gazette*, April 30, 1778; Albigence Waldo, "Diary," 315.

40. Washington, *Writings*, Revolutionary War Series 11: 348; 343; 347.

41. Washington, *Writings*, 11: 354; Cortlandt quoted in Bodle, *Valley Forge Winter*, 222; Leaven quoted in Flexner, *George Washington*, 291.

42. Washington, *Papers*, 15: 41; Flexner, *George Washington*, 291; Washington, General Orders, *Writings*, 11: 362–363.

Chapter 2. Origins and Development of the Newburgh Crisis

1. Washington, *Writings*, 26: 293.

2. Richard H. Kohn, *Eagle and Sword: The Beginnings of the Military Establishment in America.* (New York: Free Press, 1975), 123.

3. The following account relies heavily on Richard H. Kohn, "The Inside History of the Newburgh Conspiracy: America and the Coup d'Etat," *William and Mary Quarterly* 27,

no. 2 (1970): 187–220; and Paul David Nelson, *General Horatio Gates: A Biography* (Baton Rouge: Louisiana State University Press, 1976).

4. For a detailed treatment of the pension issues and related controversies, see especially Ferguson, *Power of the Purse,* chapters 1–8.

5. The English antimilitary tradition is authoritatively examined in Lois G. Schwoerer, *"No Standing Armies!": The Anti-Army Ideology in Seventeenth-Century England* (Baltimore: Johns Hopkins University Press, 1974). The American context is presented in Lawrence Delbert Cress, *Citizens in Arms: The Army and the Militia in American Society to the War of 1812* (Chapel Hill: University of North Carolina Press, 1982).

6. See Bernard Bailyn, *The Ideological Origins of the American Revolution* (Cambridge, MA: Harvard University Press, 1974), 112–119; and John Phillip Reid, *In Defiance of the Law: The Standing-Army Controversy, the Two Constitutions, and the Coming of the American Revolution (Studies in Legal History)* (Chapel Hill: University of North Carolina Press, 1981).

7. See John Shy, *Toward Lexington: The Role of the British Army in the American Revolution* (Princeton: Princeton University Press, 1965), for an expert treatment of colonial attitudes toward the British army.

8. Henry Home, Lord Kames, *Sketches of the History of Man,* ed. James A. Harris (Indianapolis: Liberty Fund, 2015), 12; *Pennsylvania Gazette,* November 30, 1758, 1; *New York Journal,* September 17, 1765, 4.

9. Hancock, *Pennsylvania Journal,* May 10, 1770, 1.

10. Cress, *Citizens in Arms,* 3–14.

11. *Pennsylvania Gazette,* December 30, 1758, 1; Lewis Nicola, quoted in Charles Royster, *A Revolutionary People at War: The Continental Army and American Character, 1775–1783* (Chapel Hill: University of North Carolina Press, 1979), 12; *Essex Journal,* September 28, 1774, 4.

12. Samuel Adams, quoted in Michael C. Desch, *Civilian Control of the Military: The Changing Security Environment* (Baltimore: Johns Hopkins University Press, 1999), 23.

13. See Carp, *Starve the Army,* generally, and Royster, *Revolutionary People at War,* 295–330.

14. Washington, *Writings,* 10: 144.

15. Smith, *Letters of Delegates,* 8: 399; 9: 707; 677; Ford, *Journals of the Continental Congress,* 10: 285–286.

16. Washington, *Writings,* 11: 237; 285.

17. Smith, *Letters of Delegates,* 8: 575; 618; 381; Clark quoted in Louis Clinton Hatch, *The Administration of the American Revolutionary Army* (New York: Macmillan, 1904), 83.

18. For an overview of the congressional debates, see Calvin Jillson and Rick K. Wilson, *Congressional Dynamics: Structure, Coordination, and Choice in the First American Congress, 1774–1789* (Stanford: Stanford University Press, 1994), 11: 502.

19. Thomas Paine, *Common Sense and The Crisis* (Garden City, NY: Anchor Books, 1973), 198; Hamilton, *Papers,* 11: 406.

20. Washington, *Writings,* 11: 15; Washington, *Papers,* 18: 398; 450.

21. For Morris's role in the half-pay controversy, see Robert Morris, *The Papers of*

Robert Morris, 1781–1784, ed. John Catanzariti (Pittsburgh: University of Pittsburgh Press, 1988), 7: 327–337; Ford, *Journals of the Continental Congress*, 17: 725.

22. Washington, *Writings*, 19: 402–413.

23. Ford, *Journals of the Continental Congress*, 17: 727; Smith, *Letters of Delegates*, 16: 236; Washington, *Writings*, 19: 484; Hamilton, *Papers*, 11: 410.

24. Smith, *Letters of Delegates*, 16: 36; 234; 264–265.

25. See Jack Rakove, *The Beginnings of National Politics: An Interpretive History of the Continental Congress* (New York: Knopf, 1979), 297–329.

26. Carp, *Starve the Army*, 204; Hamilton, *Papers*, 11: 417.

27. Rakove, *Beginnings*, 304; Merrill Jensen, *The New Nation: A History of the United States during the Confederation, 1781–1789* (New York: Vintage Books, 1950), 56; Morris quoted in Jensen, *New Nation*, 62.

28. Rakove, *Beginnings*, 297–230.

29. Rakove, *Beginnings*, 317.

30. George Washington, *A Collection of Papers, Relative to Half-pay, and Commutation of Half-pay* (Boston: Commonwealth of Massachusetts, 1783), 10–12.

31. Washington, *Collection of Papers*, 10; 11; 12; 12.

32. Morris, *Papers*, 7: 294.

33. Jillison and Wilson, *Congressional Dynamics*, 213–220.

34. Washington, *Collection of Papers*, 14.

35. Gouverneur Morris, in Morris, *Papers*, 7: 417; 417–418; Morris, *Papers*, 7: 306; Knox quoted in Richard H. Kohn, "American Generals of the Revolution: Subordination and Restraint," in *Reconsiderations on the Revolutionary War, Selected Essays*, ed. Don Higginbotham (Westport, CT: Greenwood Press, 1978), 121.

36. Washington, in *Writings*, 26: 97.

37. Hamilton, *Papers*, 3: 253–254.

38. Washington, *Writings*, 26: 186–187.

39. Madison in Smith, *Letters of Delegates*, 19: 718; 733.

40. On Gates's contested role in the Newburgh affair, see Nelson, *Horatio Gates*.

41. Washington, *Collection of Papers*, 16.

42. Washington, *Collection of Papers*, 17.

43. Washington, *Collection of Papers*, 18.

44. Washington, *Collection of Papers*, 18.

45. Washington, *Collection of Papers*, 19.

46. Washington, *Writings*, 26: 211–212; 214; 214; 216.

47. Washington, *Collection of Papers*, 20.

48. Washington, *Collection of Papers*, 20.

49. Washington, *Writings*, 26: 221.

Chapter 3. "By the dignity of your conduct"

1. Titus Livius, *The History of Rome*, "The Final Conquest of Spain," in *The History of Rome*, ed. Ernest Rhys (London: J. M. Dent and Sons, 1905), 4: 28–29.

2. For Revolutionary-era mutinies, see John H. Nagy, *Rebellion in the Ranks: Mutinies and the American Revolution* (Yardley, PA: Westholme, 2007).

3. Descriptions of the Newburgh encampment can be found in J. T. Headley, "Washington's Headquarters" and "Last Days of Washington's Army"; and Russell Headley, "Old Cantonment."

4. Washington, *Writings*, 25: 226.

5. On the rhetorical texture of revolutionary America, see Bailyn, *Ideological Origins*; and Stephen Browne, "Arts of Address in Revolutionary America," in *The SAGE Handbook of Rhetorical Studies*, ed. Andrea A. Lunsford, Kirt H. Wilson, and Rosa A. Eberly (Thousand Oaks, CA: Sage, 2009).

6. Richard R. Beeman, *The Varieties of Political Experience in Eighteenth-Century America*. (Philadelphia: University of Pennsylvania Press, 2004).

7. Gustafson, *Eloquence Is Power*, 213; see also Jay Fliegelman, *Declaring Independence: Jefferson, Natural Language, and the Culture of Performance* (Stanford: Stanford University Press, 1993), for further elaboration on this theme.

8. Samuel Adams, *The Writings of Samuel Adams*, ed. Harry Alonzo Cushing (New York: G. P. Putnam's Sons), 3: 230; George A. Billias, ed., *George Washington's Generals* (New York: Morrow, 1964).

9. Alexander McDougall, quoted in Kohn, "American Generals of the Revolution," 115; Kohn, "American Generals of the Revolution," 108.

10. Ebenezer Huntington, *Letters Written during the American Revolution* (New York: Charles Fred Hartman, 1914), 87. For a comprehensive treatment of army discontents, see Royster, *Revolutionary People at War*, 1.

11. Nickerson Hoffman, *The Turning Point of the Revolution or Burgoyne in America* (Cambridge, MA: Riverside Press, 1928), 278; Mark M. Boatner III, *Encyclopedia of the American Revolution* (New York: David McKay, 1976), 414; Flexner, *Forge*, 121.

12. The best biographical treatment of Gates is Nelson, *General Horatio Gates*.

13. On Knox, see especially Puls, *Henry Knox*.

14. North Callahan, "Henry Knox: American Artillerist," in George A. Billias, ed., *George Washington's Generals* (New York: Morrow, 1964), 239–259.

15. Sean M. Heuvel, *The Revolutionary War Memoirs of Major General William Heath* (Jefferson, NC: McFarland, 2014), for the best introduction to this overlooked but important revolutionary.

16. For Pickering on Heath, see Boatner, *Encyclopedia*, 499; for Washington on Heath, see Boatner, *Encyclopedia*, 499; Spencer on Heath quoted in Douglass Southall Freeman, *George Washington* (New York: Scribner's, 1948–1957), 4: 188.

17. George Washington, "To the Officers of the Army," referred to as the Newburgh Address, *Writings*, 26: 222–227. All citations sequential.

18. Samuel Shaw, *The Journals of Major Samuel Shaw: The First American Consul at Canton* (Boston: W. M. Crosby and H. P. Nichols, 1847), 104.

19. Resolutions, in Washington, *Collection of Papers*, 28–30.

20. James Madison, *The Papers of James Madison*, ed. William T. Hutchinson and William M. E. Rachal, vol. 6: *1 January 1783–30 April 1783* (Chicago: University of Chicago Press, 1987), 375; Elias Boudinot, in Smith, *Letters of Delegates*, 20: 74; John Francis Mercer, in Smith, *Letters of Delegates*, 20: 87.

21. Eliphet Dyer, in Smith, *Letters of Delegates,* 20: 43; congressional resolution on half pay in Washington, *Collection of Papers,* 31.

22. Washington, General Orders, *Writings,* 26: 270–72; "Farmer," *Independent Gazetteer* [Philadelphia], May 24, 1783, 2.

23. Walter Stewart, quoted in Jensen, *New Nation,* 81; on demobilization, see Jensen, *New Nation,* 54–84; and Royster, *Revolutionary People at War,* 331–368.

24. *Connecticut Current,* July 29, 1783, 1; Oliver Ellsworth in Smith, *Letters to Delegates,* 20: 228.

25. Washington to Lafayette, *Writings,* 26: 298–300.

Conclusion

1. Aristotle, *The Nicomachean Ethics,* ed. Hugh Tredennick, trans. J.A.K. Thomson (New York: Penguin, 2003).

2. Quoted in Russell F. Weigley, *The American Way of War: A History of United States Military Strategy and Policy* (Bloomington: Indiana University Press, 1973), 215.

3. Kenneth Burke, *Rhetoric of Motives* (Berkeley: University of California Press, 1969), 55.

4. Burke, *Rhetoric of Motives,* 22.

5. Aristotle quoted in George A. Kennedy, ed., *Aristotle on Rhetoric: A Theory of Civic Discourse* (New York: Oxford University Press, 1991), 37–38.

6. Richard Henry Lee, *Funeral Oration,* 2.

7. Edwin Black, "Second Persona," "Second Persona." *Quarterly Journal of Speech* 56, no. 2 (1970): 113.

8. Washington, *Writings,* 26: 216.

BIBLIOGRAPHY

Abbott, William, ed. *Memoirs of Major-General William Heath.* New York: William Abbott, 1901.

Adams, Samuel. *The Writings of Samuel Adams.* Edited by Harry Alonzo Cushing, vol. 3. New York: G. P. Putnam's Sons, 1904.

Adams, Arthur, ed. *The Hudson River in Literature.* Albany: SUNY Press, 1980.

Adams, W. Paul. "Republicanism in Political Rhetoric before 1776." *Political Science Quarterly* 85, no. 3 (1970): 397–421.

Adair, Douglass. *Fame and the Founding Fathers.* Indianapolis: Liberty Fund, 1998.

Alden, John. *The American Revolution, 1775–1783.* New York: Harper and Brothers, 1954.

———. *George Washington: A Biography.* Baton Rouge: Louisiana State University Press, 1984.

Anderson, Fred. *Crucible of War: The Seven Years' War and the Fate of Empire in British North America, 1754–1766.* New York: Knopf, 2000.

———. "The Hinge of the Revolution: George Washington Confronts a People's Army, July 3, 1775." *Massachusetts Historical Review* 1, no. 1 (1999): 20–48.

Appleby, Joyce. "Liberalism and the American Revolution." *New England Quarterly* 49, no. 1 (1976): 3–26.

Arendt, Hannah. *The Human Condition.* Chicago: University of Chicago Press, 1958.

Aristotle. *The Nicomachean Ethics.* Edited by Hugh Tredennick. Translated by J.A.K. Thomson. New York: Penguin, 2003.

Bailyn, Bernard. *The Ideological Origins of the American Revolution.* Cambridge, MA: Harvard University Press, 1974.

Baker, William S. "Itinerary of George Washington from June 1775, to December 23, 1783." *Pennsylvania Magazine of History and Biography* 15, no. 4 (1891): 394–428.

Banning, Lance. "James Madison and the Nationalists, 1780–1783." *William and Mary Quarterly* 40, no. 2 (1983): 227–255.

Beeman, Richard R. "Deference, Republicanism, and the Emergence of Popular Politics in Eighteenth-Century America." *William and Mary Quarterly* 49, no. 3 (1992): 401–430.

———. *The Varieties of Political Experience in Eighteenth-Century America.* Philadelphia: University of Pennsylvania Press, 2004.

Bickham, Troy O. "Sympathizing with Sedition? George Washington, the British Press, and British Attitudes during the American War of Independence." *William and Mary Quarterly* 59, no. 1 (2002): 101–122.

Billias, George Athan, ed. *George Washington's Generals.* New York: Morrow, 1964.

Black, Edwin. "Second Persona." *Quarterly Journal of Speech* 56, no. 2 (1970): 109–119.

Boatner, Mark M., III. *Encyclopedia of the American Revolution*. New York: David McKay, 1976.

Bodle, Wayne. "Generals and 'Gentlemen': Pennsylvania Politics and the Decision for Valley Forge." *Pennsylvania History* 62, no. 1 (1995): 59–89.

——. *The Valley Forge Winter: Civilians and Soldiers in War*. University Park: Pennsylvania State University Press, 2002.

Bowling, Kenneth R. "New Light on the Philadelphia Mutiny of 1783." *Pennsylvania Magazine of History and Biography* 101, no. 4 (1977): 419–450.

Bradley, Harold W. "The Political Thinking of George Washington." *Journal of Southern History* 11, no. 4 (1945): 469–486.

Breen, T. H. "Ideology and Nationalism on the Eve of the American Revolution: Revisions Once More in Need of Revising." *Journal of American History* 84, no. 1 (1997): 13–39.

Brenneman, Gloria. "The Conway Cabal: Myth or Reality." *Pennsylvania History* 40, no. 2 (1973): 168–177.

Browne, Stephen. "Arts of Address in Revolutionary America." In *The SAGE Handbook of Rhetorical Studies*, edited by Andrea A. Lunsford, Kirt H. Wilson, and Rosa A. Eberly, 230–245. Thousand Oaks: SAGE, 2009.

Burke, Kenneth. *Rhetoric of Motives*. Berkeley: University of California Press, 1969.

Burnett, Edmund C., ed. *Letters of Members of the Continental Congress*. 8 vols. Washington, DC: Carnegie Institute of Washington, 1921–36.

Burstein, Andrew. "The Political Character of Sympathy." *Journal of the Early Republic* 21, no. 4 (2001): 601–632.

Carp, E. Wayne. "The Origins of the Nationalist Movement of 1780–1783: Congressional Administration and the Continental Army." *Pennsylvania Magazine of History and Biography* 107, no. 3 (1983): 363–392.

——. *To Starve the Army at Pleasure*. Chapel Hill: University of North Carolina Press, 1984.

Chernow, Ron. *Washington: A Life*. New York: Penguin, 2010.

Chrissanthos, Stefan G. "Scipio and the Mutiny at Sucro, 206 B.C." *Historia Zeitschrift für Alte Geschichte* 46, no. 2 (1997): 172–184.

Cox, Caroline. "The Continental Army." In *The Oxford Handbook of the American Revolution*, edited by Edward G. Gray and Jane Kamensky, 161–176. New York: Oxford University Press, 2013.

——. *A Proper Sense of Honor: Service and Sacrifice in George Washington's Army*. Chapel Hill: University of North Carolina Press, 2004.

Cress, Lawrence Delbert. *Citizens in Arms: The Army and the Militia in American Society to the War of 1812*. Chapel Hill: University of North Carolina Press, 1982.

——. "Republican Liberty and National Security: American Military Policy as an Ideological Problem, 1783–1789." *William and Mary Quarterly* 38, no. 1 (1981): 73–96.

Cunliffe, Marcus. *George Washington: Man and Monument*. Boston: Little, Brown, 1982.

——. *Soldiers and Civilians: The Martial Spirit in America, 1775–1865*. Boston: Little, Brown, 1968.

Dearborn, Henry. *Revolutionary War Journals of Henry Dearborn*. Edited by Lloyd A. Brown and Howard H. Peckham. Chicago: Caxton Club, 1939.

Desch, Michael C. *Civilian Control of the Military: The Changing Security Environment.* Baltimore: John Hopkins University Press, 1999.

Dreisback, Daniel L. "The 'Vine and Fig Tree' in George Washington's Letters: Reflections on a Biblical Motif in the Literature of the American Founding Era." *Anglican and Episcopal History* 76, no. 3 (2007): 299–326.

Elkins, Stanley, and Eric McKitrick. *The Age of Federalism: The Early American Republic, 1788–1800.* New York: Oxford University Press, 1993.

Ellis, Joseph J. "The Farewell: Washington's Wisdom at the End." In *George Washington Reconsidered,* edited by Don Higginbotham, 212–249. Charlottesville: University Press of Virginia, 2001.

———. *His Excellency: George Washington.* New York: Knopf, 2004.

Engal, Marc. "The Origins of the Revolution in Virginia: A Reinterpretation." *William and Mary Quarterly* 37, no. 3 (1980): 401–428.

Everett, Oliver. *An Eulogy, on General George Washington.* Charlestown, MA: Samuel Etheridge, 1800.

Ferguson, E. James. "The Nationalists of 1781–1783 and the Economic Interpretation of the Constitution." *Journal of American History* 56, no. 2 (1969): 241–261.

———. *The Power of the Purse: A History of American Public Finance, 1776–1790.* Chapel Hill: University of North Carolina Press, 1961.

Ferguson, Robert A. *The American Enlightenment, 1750–1820.* Cambridge, MA: Harvard University Press, 1997.

Ferling, John E. *The First of Men: A Life of George Washington.* Knoxville: University of Tennessee Press, 1988.

Ferling, John E., ed. *The World Turned Upside Down: The American Victory in the War of Independence.* Westport, CT: Greenwood Press, 1988.

Flexner, James Thomas. *George Washington.* 4 vols. Boston: Little, Brown, 1965–1972.

———. *George Washington: The Forge of Experience, 1732–1775.* Boston: Little, Brown, 1965.

———. *Washington: The Indispensable Man.* New York: Signet, 1984.

Fishman, Ethan, William D. Pederson, and Mark J. Rozell, eds. *George Washington: Foundation of Presidential Leadership and Character.* Westport,CT: Praeger, 2001.

Fliegelman, Jay. *Declaring Independence: Jefferson, Natural Language, and the Culture of Performance.* Stanford: Stanford University Press, 1993.

Ford, Worthington C., et al. *Journals of the Continental Congress, 1774–1789.* 34 vols. Washington, DC: US Government Printing Office, 1904–37.

Freeman, Douglas Southall. *George Washington.* 7 vols. New York: Scribner's, 1948–1957.

Furlong, Patrick J. "A Sermon for the Mutinous Troops of the Connecticut Line, 1782." *New England Quarterly* 43, no. 4 (1970): 621–631.

Furstenberg, Francois. "Beyond Freedom and Slavery: Autonomy, Virtue, and Resistance in Early American Political Discourse." *Journal of American History* 89, no. 4 (2003): 1295–1330.

Furtwangler, Albert. *American Silhouettes: Rhetorical Identities of the Founders.* New Haven: Yale University Press, 1987.

Gallagher, Mary A. Y. "Reinterpreting the 'Very Trifling Mutiny' at Philadelphia in June 1783." *Pennsylvania Magazine of History and Biography* 119, no. 1/2 (1995): 3–35.

Glasson, William H. *Federal Military Pensions in the United States*. New York: Oxford University Press, 1918.

Gray, Edward G., and Jane Kamensky, eds. *The Oxford Handbook of the American Revolution*. New York: Oxford University Press, 2013.

Gustafson, Sandra. *Eloquence Is Power: Oratory and Performance in Early America*. Chapel Hill: University of North Carolina Press, 2000.

Haggard, Robert F. "The Nicola Affair: Lewis Nicola, George Washington, and American Military Discontent during the Revolutionary War." *Proceedings of the American Philosophical Society* 146, no. 2 (2002): 139–169.

Hallam, John S. "Houdon's Washington in Richmond: Some New Observations." *American Art Journal* 10, no. 2 (1978): 72–80.

Hamilton, Alexander. *The Papers of Alexander Hamilton*. Edited by H. C. Syrett et al. 26 vols. New York: Columbia University Press, 1961–79.

Hancock, John. *Pennsylvania Journal*. May 10, 1770, 1.

Hatch, Louis Clinton. *The Administration of the American Revolutionary Army*. New York: Macmillan, 1904.

Headley, J. T. "Last Days of Washington's Army at Newburgh." *Harper's New Monthly Magazine* 67 (October 1883): 651–672.

——. "Washington's Headquarters at Newburgh." *Galaxy* 22, no. 1 (1876): 7–21.

Headley, Russell. "The Old Cantonment at Newburgh. *New England Magazine* 19, no. 5 (1896): 578–593.

Henderson, H. James. *Party Politics in the Continental Congress*. New York: McGraw-Hill, 1974.

Henriques, Peter R. *Realistic Visionary: A Portrait of George Washington*. Charlottesville: University of Virginia Press, 2008.

Herrera, Ricardo A. "Self-Governance and the American Citizen as Soldier, 1775–1861." *Journal of Military History* 65, no. 1 (2001): 21–52.

Heuvel, Sean M. *The Revolutionary War Memoirs of Major General William Heath*. Jefferson, NC: McFarland, 2014.

Higginbotham, Don. "American Historian and the Military History of the American Revolution." *American Historical Review* 70, no. 1 (1964): 18–34.

——. "The Early American Way of War: Reconnaissance and Appraisal." *William and Mary Quarterly* 44, no. 2 (1987): 230–273.

——. *George Washington and the American Military Tradition*. Athens: University of Georgia Press, 1985.

——. *George Washington: Uniting a Nation*. New York: Rowman and Littlefield, 2002.

——. *The War of American Independence: Military Attitudes, Policies, and Practices, 1763–1789*. New York: Macmillan, 1971.

Higginbotham, Don, ed. *George Washington Reconsidered*. Charlottesville: University Press of Virginia, 2001.

——, ed. *Reconsiderations on the Revolutionary War: Selected Essays*. Westport, CT: Greenwood Press, 1978.

Hoffman, Nickerson. *The Turning Point of the Revolution or Burgoyne in America*. Cambridge, MA: Riverside Press, 1928.

Hoffmann, Ronald, and Peter J. Albert, eds. *Arms and Independence: The Military Character of the American Revolution.* Charlottesville: University Press of Virginia, 1984.

Home, Henry, Lord Kames. *Sketches of the History of Man.* Edited by James A. Harris. Indianapolis: Liberty Fund, 2015.

Huntington, Ebenezer. *Letters Written during the American Revolution.* New York: Charles Fred Hartman, 1914.

Huntington, Samuel P. *The Soldier and the State: The Theory and Politics of Civil-Military Relations.* Cambridge, MA: Harvard University Press, 1957.

Isaac, Rhys. *The Transformation of Virginia, 1740–1790.* Chapel Hill: University of North Carolina Press, 1982.

Jacobs, James Ripley. *The Beginnings of the US Army, 1783–1812.* Princeton: Princeton University Press, 1947.

Jackson, Andrew. *Papers of Andrew Jackson.* Edited by Harold D. Mores and J. Clint Cliff. Knoxville: University of Tennessee Press, 2002.

Jensen, Merrill. "The American People and the American Revolution." *Journal of American History* 57, no. 1 (1970): 5–35.

———. *The New Nation: A History of the United States during the Confederation, 1781–1789.* New York: Vintage Books, 1950.

Jillson, Calvin, and Rick K. Wilson. *Congressional Dynamics: Structure, Coordination, and Choice in the First American Congress, 1774–1789.* Stanford: Stanford University Press, 1994.

Johnson, John B. *Eulogy on General Washington.* Albany, NY: L. Andrews, 1800.

Kallich, Martin, and Andrew MacLeish, eds. *The American Revolution through British Eyes.* New York: Harper and Row, 1962.

Kaplan, Sidney. "Rank and Status among Massachusetts Continental Officers." *American Historical Review* 56, no. 2 (1951): 318–326.

———. "Veteran Officers and Politics in Massachusetts, 1783–1787." *William and Mary Quarterly* 9, no. 1 (1952): 29–57.

Kennedy, George A. *Aristotle on Rhetoric: A Theory of Civic Discourse.* New York: Oxford University Press, 1991.

Knollenberg, Bernhard. *George Washington: The Virginia Period, 1732–1775.* Durham, NC: Duke University Press, 1964.

———. *Washington and the Revolution: A Reappraisal.* New York: Macmillan, 1940.

Kohn, Richard H. "American Generals of the Revolution: Subordination and Restraint." In *Reconsiderations on the Revolutionary War, Selected Essays,* edited by Don Higginbotham, 104–23. Westport,CT: Greenwood Press, 1978.

———. *Eagle and Sword: The Beginnings of the Military Establishment in America.* New York: Free Press, 1975.

———. "The Inside History of the Newburgh Conspiracy: America and the Coup d'Etat." *William and Mary Quarterly* 27, no. 2 (1970): 187–220.

———. "The Social History of the American Soldier: A Review and Prospectus for Research." *American Historical Review* 86, no. 3 (1981): 553–567.

Leach, Douglas Edward. *Arms for Empire: A Military History of the British Colonies in North America, 1607–1763.* New York: Macmillan, 1973.

Lee, Richard Henry. *A Funeral Oration*. Philadelphia: John Ormond, 1799.

Lee, Wayne E. "Early American Ways of War: A New Reconnaissance, 1600–1815." *Historical Journal* 44, no. 1 (2001): 269–289.

Leibiger, Stuart. "'To Judge of Washington's Conduct': Illuminating George Washington's Appearance on the World Stage." *Virginia Magazine of History and Biography* 107, no. 1 (1999): 37–44.

Liell, Scott. *Forty-Six Pages*. Philadelphia: Running Press, 2003.

Livius, Titus. "The Final Conquest of Spain." *The History of Rome*, Vol. 4. Edited by Ernest Rhys. London: J. M. Dent and Sons, 1905.

Longmore, Paul K. *The Invention of George Washington*. Berkeley: University of California Press, 1988.

Loss, Richard. "The Political Thought of President George Washington." *Presidential Studies Quarterly* 19, no. 3 (1989): 471–490.

Lucas, Stephen E. "Genre Criticism and Historical Context: The Case of George Washington's First Inaugural Address." *Southern Speech Journal* 51, no. 4 (1986): 354–370.

———. *Portents of Rebellion: Rhetoric and Revolution in Philadelphia, 1765–76*. Philadelphia: Temple University Press, 1976.

Mackesy, Piers. *The War for America, 1775–1783*. Cambridge, MA: Harvard University Press, 1964.

Madison, James. *The Papers of James Madison,* edited by William T. Hutchinson and William M. E. Rachal. Vol. 6: *1 January 1783–30 April 1783*. Chicago: University of Chicago Press, 1987.

Martin, James Kirby. "The Continental Army and the American Victory." In *The World Turned Upside Down*, edited by John Ferling, 19–34. Westport, CT: Greenwood Press, 1988.

Martin, James Kirby, and Mark E. Lender. *A Respectable Army: The Military Origins of the Republic, 1763–1789*. Arlington Heights, Ill.: Harlan Davidson, 1982.

Mauerer, Maurer. "Military Justice under General Washington. *Military Affairs* 28, no. 2 (1964–65): 8–16.

Mayo, Bernard. "George Washington." *Georgia Review* 13, no. 3 (1959): 135–150.

McDonald, Forrest. *E Pluribus Unum: The Formation of the American Republic, 1776–1790*. Boston: Houghton Mifflin, 1965.

Middlekauf, Robert. *The Glorious Cause: The American Revolution, 1763–1789*. New York: Oxford University Press, 1982.

———. "Why Men Fought in the American Revolution." *Huntington Library Quarterly* 43, no. 2 (1980): 135–148.

Mihm, Stephen. "Funding the Revolution: Monetary and Fiscal Policy in Eighteenth-Century America." In *The Oxford Handbook of the American Revolution,* edited by Edward G. Gray and Jane Kamensky, 327–351. New York: Oxford University Press, 2013.

Minot, George Richards. *Eulogy on George Washington.*" Boston: Manning and Loring, 1800.

Montgomery, H. C. "Washington the Stoic." *Classical Journal* 31, no. 6 (1936): 371–373.

Morgan, Edmund S. *The Genius of George Washington*. New York: Norton, 1980.

———. "George Washington: The Aloof American." In *George Washington Reconsidered,* edited by Don Higginbotham, 287–308. Charlottesville: University Press of Virginia, 2001.

Morris, Robert. *The Papers of Robert Morris, 1781–1784*. Vol. 7. Edited by John Catanzariti. Pittsburgh: University of Pittsburgh Press, 1988.

Nagy, John H. *Rebellion in the Ranks: Mutinies and the American Revolution*. Yardley, PA: Westholme, 2007.

Nelson, Paul David. "Citizen Soldiers or Regulars: The Views of American General Officers on the Military Establishment, 1775–1781." *Military Affairs* 43, no. 3 (1979): 126–132.

——. *General Horatio Gates: A Biography*. Baton Rouge: Louisiana State University Press, 1976.

——. "Horatio Gates at Newburgh, 1783: A Misunderstood Role." *William and Mary Quarterly* 29, no. 1 (1972): 143–158.

Nettles, Curtis P. *George Washington and American Independence*. Boston: Little, Brown, 1951.

Newcomb, Benjamin. "Washington's Generals and the Decision to Quarter at Valley Forge." *Pennsylvania Magazine of History and Biography* 117, no. 4 (1993): 309–329.

Newman, Simon P. "Principles or Men? George Washington and the Political Culture of National Leadership, 1776–1801." *Journal of the Early Republic* 12, no. 4 (1992): 477–507.

Padover, Saul. "George Washington—Portrait of a True Conservative." *Social Research* 22, no. 2 (1955): 199–222.

Paine, Thomas. *Common Sense and The Crisis*. Garden City, NY: Anchor Books, 1973.

——. *On the Life of George Washington*. Newburyport, MA: Edmund M. Blunt, January 2, 1800.

Pavlosky, Arnold M. "'Between Hawk and Buzzard': Congress as Perceived by Its Members, 1775–1783." *Pennsylvania Magazine of History and Biography* 101, no. 3 (1977): 349–364.

Phelps, Glenn A. *George Washington and American Constitutionalism*. Lawrence: University Press of Kansas, 1993.

Puls, Mark. *Henry Knox: Visionary General of the American Revolution*. New York: Palgrave Macmillan, 2008.

Purcell, Sarah J. *Sealed with Blood: War, Sacrifice, and Memory in Revolutionary America*. Philadelphia: University of Pennsylvania Press, 2002.

Rakove, Jack. *The Beginnings of National Politics: An Interpretive History of the Continental Congress*. New York: Knopf, 1979.

——. *Revolutionaries: A New History of the Invention of America*. New York: Houghton Mifflin, 2011.

Ramsey, David. *The History of the American Revolution*. Edited by Lester H. Cohen. Indianapolis: Liberty Classics, 1990.

Rankin, Hugh. "Washington's Lieutenants and the American Victory." In *The World Upside Down*, edited by John Ferling, 71–90. Westport, CT: Greenwood Press, 1988.

Ray, John. "George Washington's Pre-Presidential Statesmanship, 1783–1789." *Presidential Studies Quarterly* 27, no. 2 (1997): 207–220.

Reid, John Phillip. *In Defiance of the Law: The Standing-Army Controversy, the Two Constitutions, and the Coming of the American Revolution (Studies in Legal History)*. Chapel Hill: University of North Carolina Press, 1981.

Rossie, Jonathan Gregory. *The Politics of Command in the American Revolution*. Syracuse: Syracuse University Press, 1975.

Royster, Charles. *A Revolutionary People at War: The Continental Army and American Character, 1775–1783.* Chapel Hill: University of North Carolina Press, 1979.

Sayen, William Guthrie. "George Washington's 'Unmannerly' Behavior: The Clash between Civility and Honor." *Virginia Magazine of History and Biography* 107, no. 1 (1999): 5–36.

Schwartz, Barry. "George Washington and the Whig Conception of Heroic Leadership." *American Sociological Review* 48, no. 1 (1983): 18–33.

———. *George Washington: The Making of an American Symbol.* New York: Free Press, 1987.

Schwoerer, Lois G. *"No Standing Armies!": The Anti-Army Ideology in Seventeenth-Century England.* Baltimore: Johns Hopkins University Press, 1974.

Seabury, Paul. "Provisionality and Finality." *Annals of the American Academy of Political and Social Science* 392 (November 1970): 96–104.

Shalhope, Robert E. "The Armed Citizen in the Early Republic." *Law and Contemporary Problems* 49, no. 1 (1986): 125–141.

Shaw, Samuel. *The Journals of Major Samuel Shaw: The First American Consul at Canton.* Boston: W. M. Crosby and H. P. Nichols, 1847.

Shy, John. "The American Military Experience: History and Learning." *Journal of Interdisciplinary History* 1, no. 2 (1971): 205–228.

———. "The American Revolution: The Military Conflict Considered as a Revolutionary War." In *Essays on the American Revolution,* edited by Stephen G. Kurtz and James H. Hutson, 121–156. Chapel Hill: University of North Carolina Press, 1973.

———. "American Society and Its War for Independence." In *Reconsiderations on the Revolutionary War: Selected Essays,* edited by Don Higginbotham, 72–82. Westport, CT: Greenwood Press, 1978.

———. "The Cultural Approach to the History of War." *Journal of Military History* 57, no. 1 (1993): 13–26.

———. "A New Look at the Colonial Militia." *William and Mary Quarterly* 20, no. 2 (1963): 175–185.

———. *A People Numerous and Armed: Reflections on the Military Struggle for American Independence.* Ann Arbor: University of Michigan Press, 1990.

———. *Toward Lexington: The Role of the British Army in the American Revolution.* Princeton: Princeton University Press, 1965.

Skeen, C. Edward, and Richard H. Kohn. "The Newburgh Conspiracy Reconsidered." *William and Mary Quarterly* 31, no. 2 (1974): 273–298.

Skelton, William B. "Social Roots of the American Military Profession: The Officer Corps of America's First Peacetime Army, 1784–1789." *Journal of Military History* 54, no. 4 (1990): 435–452.

Smith, Paul H, ed. *Letters of Delegates to Congress.* 24 vols. Washington, DC: Library of Congress, 1976–2000.

Smith, Richard Norton. *Patriarch: George Washington and the New American Nation.* New York: Houghton Mifflin, 1993.

Sweig, Donald M. "A New-Found Washington Letter of 1774 and the Fairfax Resolves." *William and Mary Quarterly* 40, no. 2 (1983): 285.

Tate, Thad W. "The Coming of the Revolution in Virginia: Britain's Challenge to Virginia's Ruling Class, 1763–1776." *William and Mary Quarterly* 19, no. 3 (1962): 323–343.

Taylor, Alan. "From Fathers to Friends of the People: Political Personas in the Early Republic." *Journal of the Early Republic* 11, no. 4 (1991): 465–491.

Trees, Andrew S. *The Founding Fathers and the Politics of Character.* Princeton: Princeton University Press, 2004.

Waldo, Albigence. "Valley Forge, 1777–1778. Diary of Surgeon Albigence Waldo, of the Connecticut Line." *Pennsylvania Magazine of History and Biography* 21, no. 3 (1897): 299–323.

Waldstreicher, David. *'In the Midst of Perpetual Fetes': The Making of American Nationalism, 1776–1820.* Chapel Hill: University of North Carolina Press, 1997.

Warner, Michael. *The Letters of the Republic: Publication and the Public Sphere in Eighteenth-Century America.* Cambridge, MA: Harvard University Press, 1900.

Warren, Mercy Otis. *History of the Rise, Progress and Termination of the American Revolution.* Edited by Lester H. Cohen. Indianapolis: Liberty Classics, 1988.

Washington, George. *A Collection of Papers, Relative to Half-pay, and Commutation of Half-pay.* Boston: Commonwealth of Massachusetts, 1783.

——. *The Journal of Major George Washington.* Williamsburg, VA: William Hunter, 1754.

——. *The Papers of George Washington: Colonial Series.* Edited by W. W. Abbot. 7 vols. to date. Charlottesville: University Press of Virginia, 1983–.

——. *The Papers of George Washington: Revolutionary War Series.* Edited by Philander D. Chase. 4 vols. to date. Charlottesville: University Press of Virginia, 1985–.

——. *Writings of George Washington.* Edited by John C. Fitzpatrick. Washington, DC: US Government Printing Office, 1931–1944.

Weigley, Russell F. *The American Way of War: A History of United States Military Strategy and Policy.* Bloomington: Indiana University Press, 1973.

Weir, Robert M. "Who Shall Rule at Home: The American Revolution as a Crisis of Legitimacy for the Colonial Elite." *Journal of Interdisciplinary History* 6, no. 4 (1976): 679–700.

Wills, Garry. *Cincinnatus: George Washington and the Enlightenment.* Garden City, NY: Doubleday, 1984.

Wilson, Woodrow. *George Washington.* New York: Schocken, 1969.

Winterer, Caroline. "From Royal to Republican: The Classical Image in Early America." *Journal of American History* 91, no. 4 (2005): 1264–1290.

Wood, Gordon. "Conspiracy and the Paranoid Style: Causality and Deceit in the Eighteenth Century." *William and Mary Quarterly* 39, no. 3 (1982): 401–441.

——. *The Creation of the American Republic, 1776–1787.* Chapel Hill: University of North Carolina Press, 1969.

——. "The Greatness of George Washington." In *George Washington Reconsidered,* edited by Don Higginbotham, 309–324. Charlottesville: University Press of Virginia, 2001.

——. *The Radicalism of the American Revolution.* New York: Knopf, 1992.

Zuckerman, Michael. "The Polite and the Plebian." In *The Oxford Handbook of the American Revolution,* edited by Edward G. Gray and Jane Kamensky, 47–63. New York: Oxford University Press, 2013.

INDEX

Adams, John, 3, 13
Adams, Samuel, 34, 48, 72, 74
Alden, John R., 4, 30, 34
Arendt, Hannah, 23
Aristotle, 96–100, 102
Armstrong, John, 62

Bailyn, Bernard, 72
beginnings, 22–29, 39, 73
Black, Edwin, 101
Boudinot, Elias, 90
Braddock, Edward, 29–30, 32–33
Brooks, John, 56–58, 62, 89
Burgh, James, 47, 95
Burke, Kenneth, 98–99

Caesar, Julius, 5, 45
character, 4–7, 14, 20–42, 67, 85–87, 89, 92, 99–102
Chastellux, Marquis, 4, 70
Cincinnatus, 17, 25
Circular Letter to the States (1783), 13, 14, 25, 70, 88, 94
commutation, 44, 59, 66, 90–91
conspiracy, 1, 3, 35, 43, 66, 76, 79–81, 89
Continental Army, 1, 6, 8, 43
Continental Congress, 8, 12, 22
Cromwell, Oliver, 45–46
Cunliffe, Marcus, 4

Dinwiddie, Robert, 27–32
Drama, 15, 19–25, 73, 78–79, 86, 102–4
Dunmore, John Murray, Earl of, 34
Dyer, Eliphet, 90

Ellis, Joseph, 25
endings, 25–29, 73
ethos, 4, 6, 100

Fabius Maximus, 5, 67–68
Fairfax, Bryan, 35–37
Fairfax Resolutions, 35
Farewell Address (Washington), 13, 25, 88, 94
First Inaugural Address (Washington), 13, 88, 94
Fitzhugh, William, 31
Flexnor, James Thomas, 2, 14, 30, 34–36
Fort Necessity, 29, 97
Franklin, Benjamin, 3, 40, 58

Gates, Henry, 2, 7, 49, 62, 64, 73, 75–77, 90–91, 118
Gerry, Elbridge, 18–19, 49–50
Greene, Nathanael, 40, 70, 73–74
Gustafson, Sandra, 73

half-pay controversy, 16, 44, 49–54, 66, 90–91
Hamilton, Alexander, 3, 13, 18, 52–56, 60–61, 66, 70, 84, 103
Heath, William, 16, 59, 70, 77–78
Henry, Patrick, 13, 35, 39, 72–73
Higginbotham, Don, 10, 30
House of Burgesses, 2, 28, 33, 34, 95

identification, 8, 40, 42, 74, 83, 98–99

Jackson, Andrew, 24–25
Jefferson, Thomas, 3, 5, 12–13, 17, 26, 72
Jensen, Merrill, 55
Jones, Joseph, 49, 65
Jumonville affair, 24, 29

Knox, Henry, 2, 7, 10, 18, 56–59, 70, 73–74, 76–77, 89
Kohn, Richard H., 18, 43, 74, 93

Lafayette, Marquis de, 70, 73, 92
Laurens, Henry, 40, 50
Laurens, John, 41
Lee, Charles, 21, 73, 75
Lee, Richard Henry, 22, 35, 100
Lovell, James, 50, 54

Madison, James, 3, 14, 58, 61–62, 72, 90
Marshall, George C. 96–98
Mason, George, 3, 34–35
McDougall, William, 2, 56–59, 74
Memorial from Officers of the Army, 52, 56–58
Middlekauff, Robert, 3, 93
Mifflin, Thomas, 49
Morgan, Edmund S. 33, 39
Morris, Gouverneur, 49, 53, 55, 59
Morris, Robert, 49, 52–53, 55–56, 58–60, 66
Mount Vernon, 1, 3, 25, 32, 34, 60
mutiny, 43, 54, 58–59, 69, 71, 83, 91

Newburgh Address, 3, 12–14, 67–72, 79–94, 99–103
Newburgh, New York, 1, 70
Nicola, Lewis, 70

Ogden, Mathias, 56, 58
oratory, 12, 73
Orme, Robert, 31–33

Paine, Thomas, 13, 22, 23, 51, 72, 88
pensions, 16–19, 44, 54, 57, 74–75
Pickering, Timothy, 2, 18, 49, 77
promises, 6, 23–25, 29

Rakove, Jack, 55–56
rhetoric, 4, 6, 11–15, 25, 68, 71–73, 94–103
ritual, 7, 11, 15, 26, 38–40, 42, 102

Scipio, 69, 97
Shaw, Samuel, 89
Shy, John, 15
Society of the Cincinnati, 7, 19
standing army, 19, 46–48
Steuben, Baron von, 18, 40, 70
Stewart, Walter, 62, 91

temple (Newburgh structure), 11, 44, 62, 64, 66, 70, 78, 103
Trumbull, Jonathan, 49, 90

Valley Forge, 9–10, 37–42, 50, 52, 67, 74
virtue, 5–7, 17, 20–21, 27, 46–47, 52–54, 63, 75, 87–92, 96, 99, 104, 118

Washington, George: and character, 4–7, 20–42, 85–87, 99–102; characterizations of, by Alden, 4, by Cunliffe, 4, by Ellis, 25, by Flexnor, 35, by Jefferson, 26–27, by Morgan, 33, 39; compared to Caesar, 5, 45, Cincinnatus, 17, 25, Fabius, 5, 67–68, Marshall, 96–98, Scipio, 69, 97; and conspiracy rhetoric, 79–81; and commutation, 90–91; and Cromwell, 45–46; and Gates, 75–77; and Greene and Hamilton, 52–56, 60–61; and Jumonville affair, 24, 29; and Lafayette, 70, 73, 92; nature of beginnings, 22–29; nature of endings, 25–29; and Newburgh Address, 3, 12–14, 67–72, 79–94, 99–103; and Society of the Cincinnati, 7, 19; and Valley Forge, 9–10, 37–42; and virtue, 52–54, 87–92
Williamsburg, 28, 34
Wills, Gary, 25